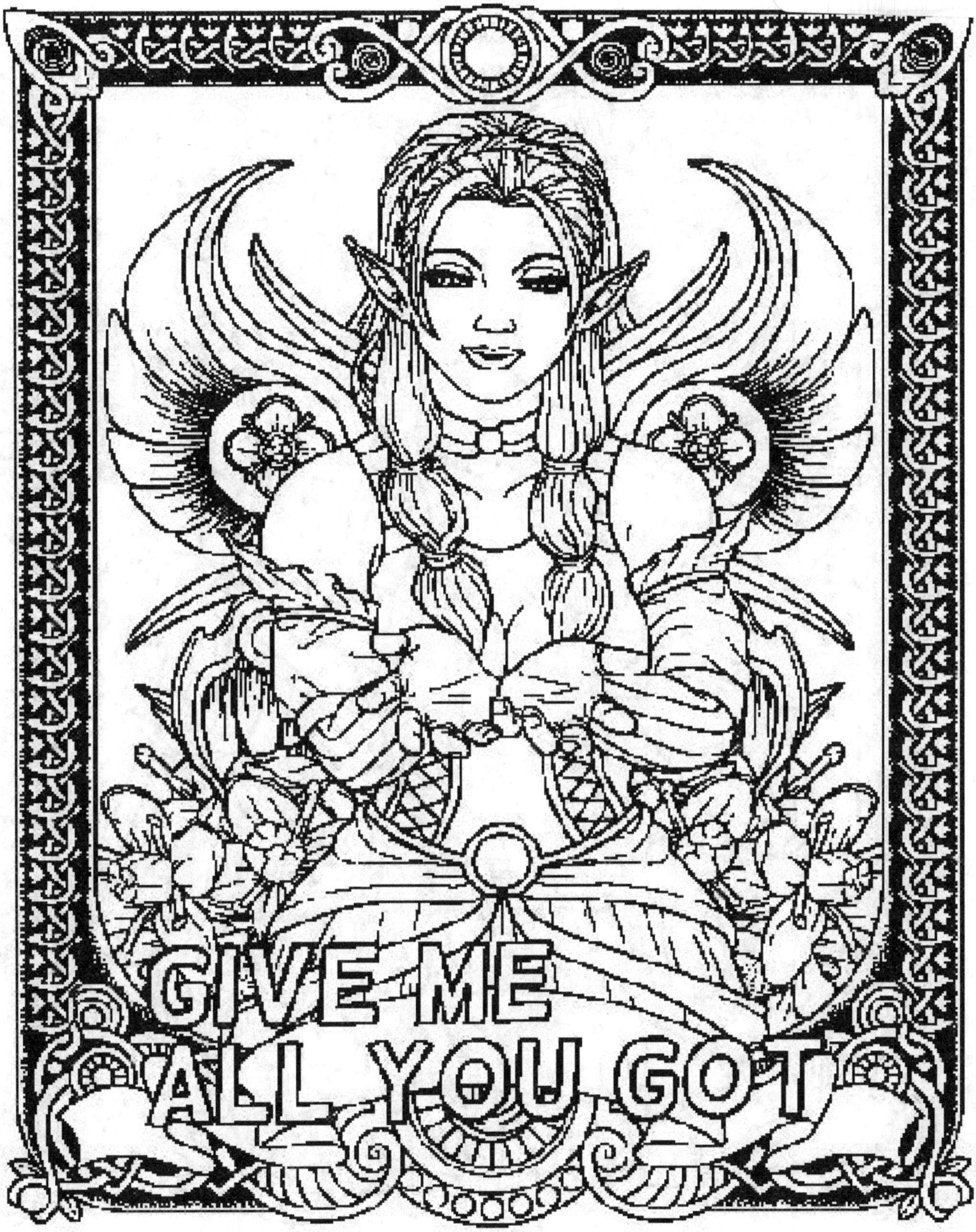
GIVE ME
ALL YOU GOT

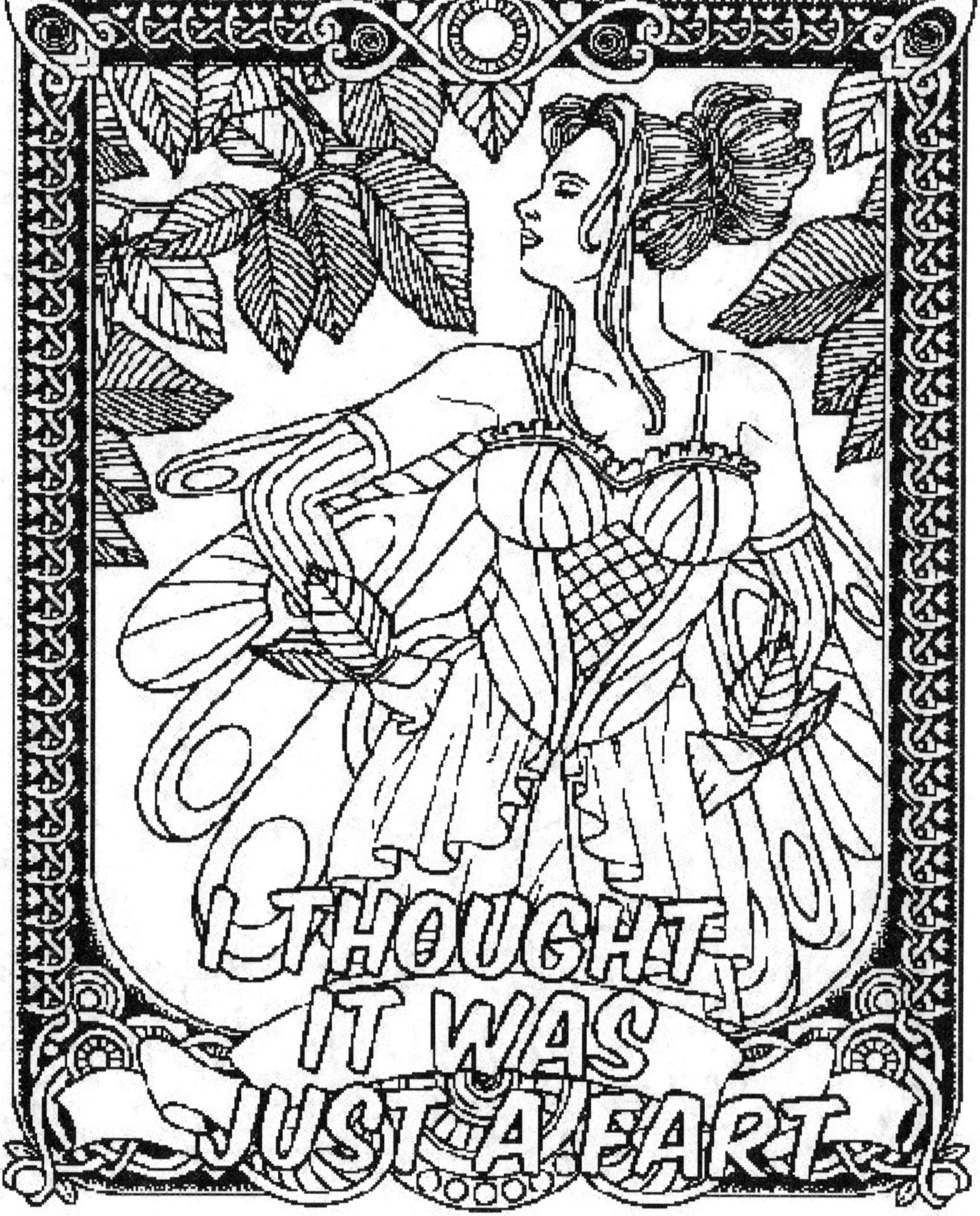
I THOUGHT
IT WAS
JUST A FART

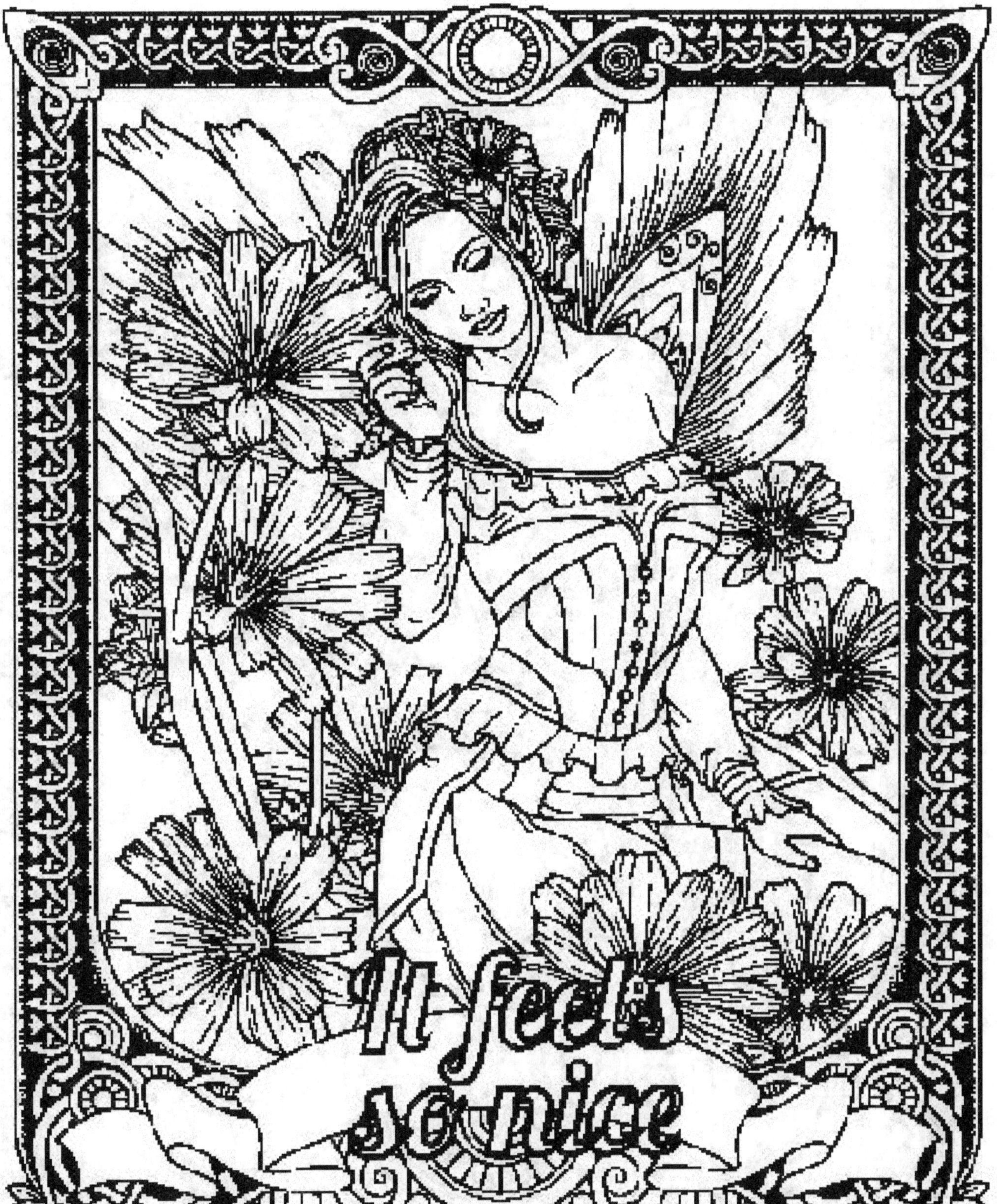
It feels
so nice

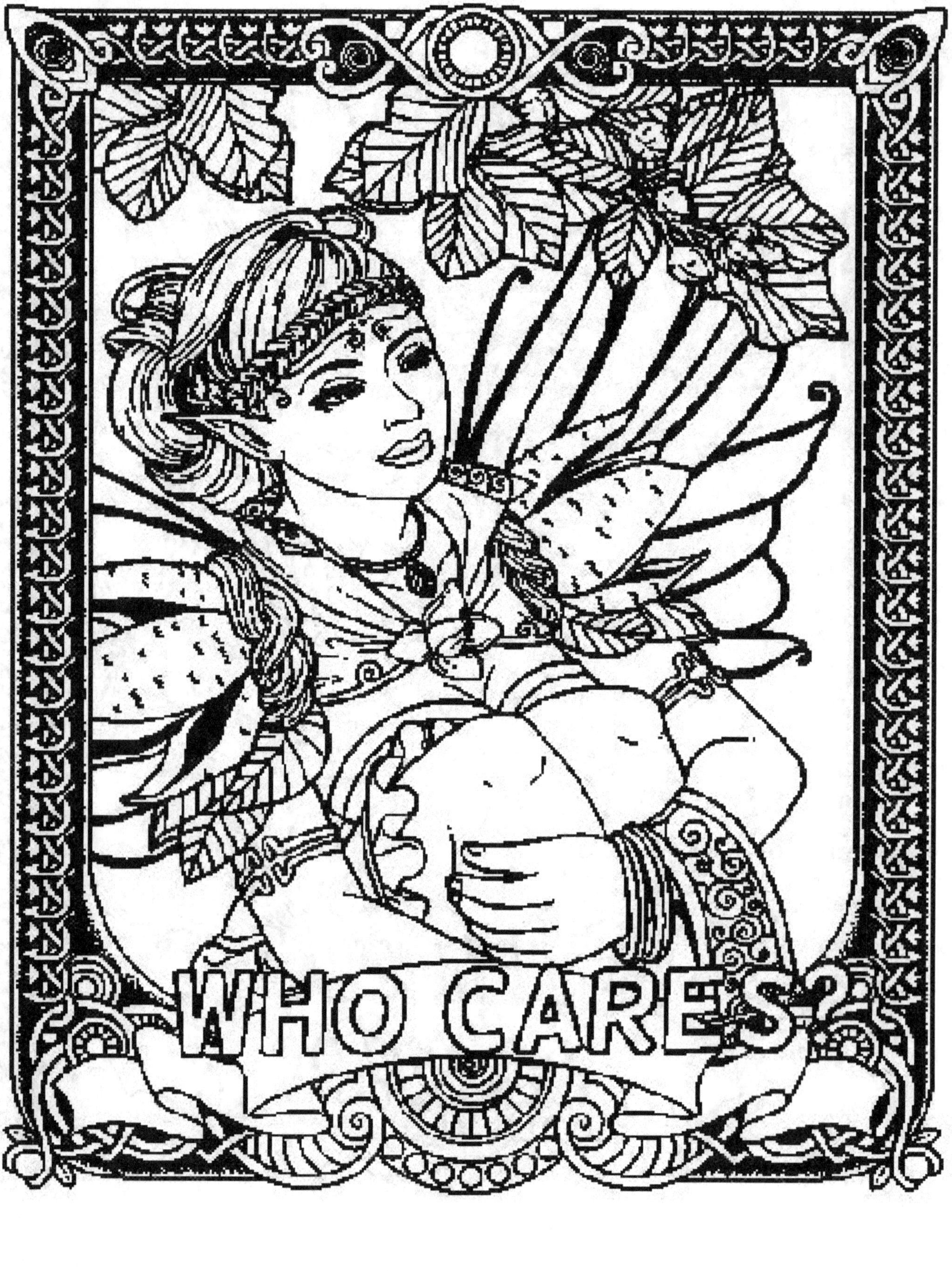
WHO CARES?

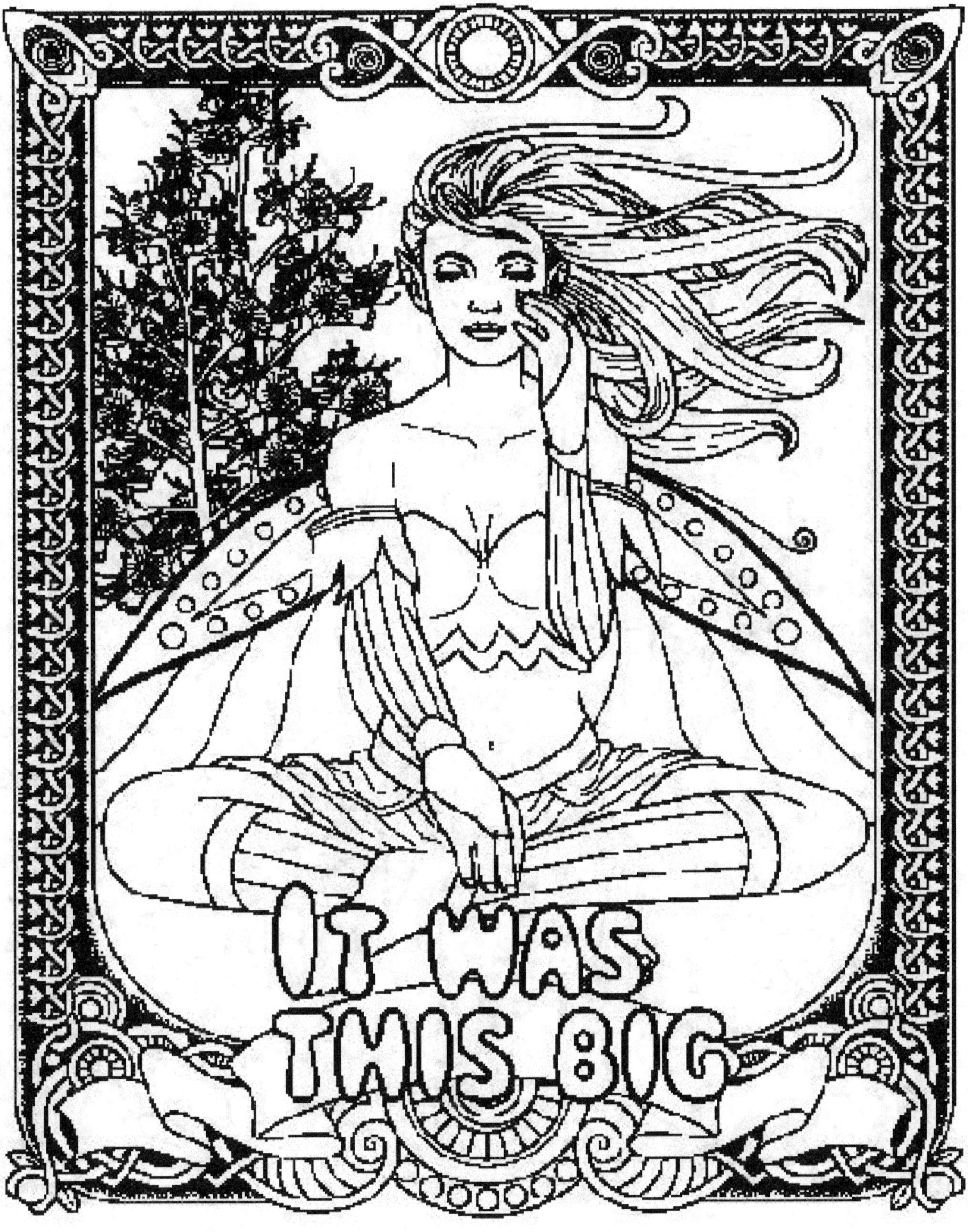
IT WAS
THIS BIG

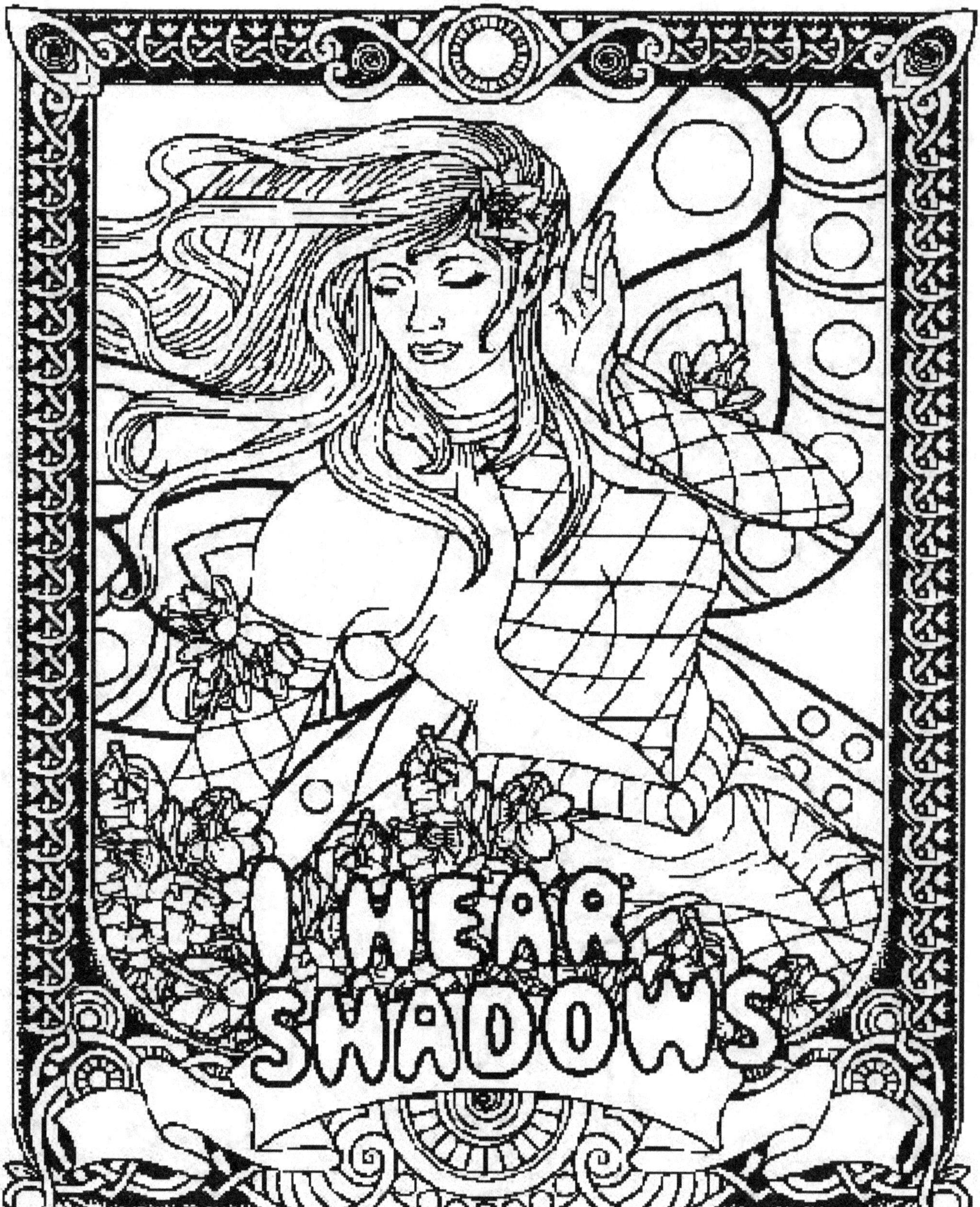
I HEAR
SHADOWS

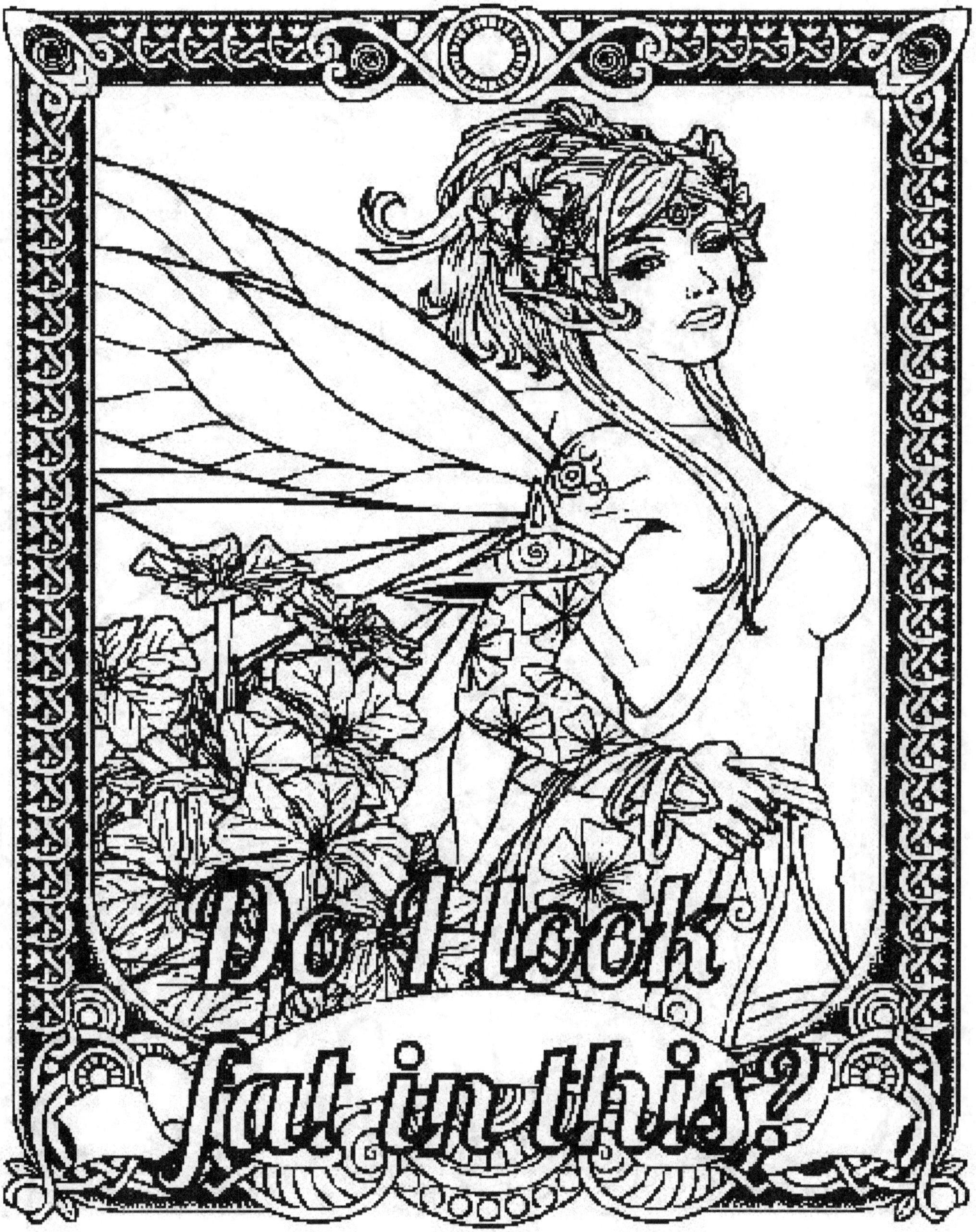
Do I look
fat in this?

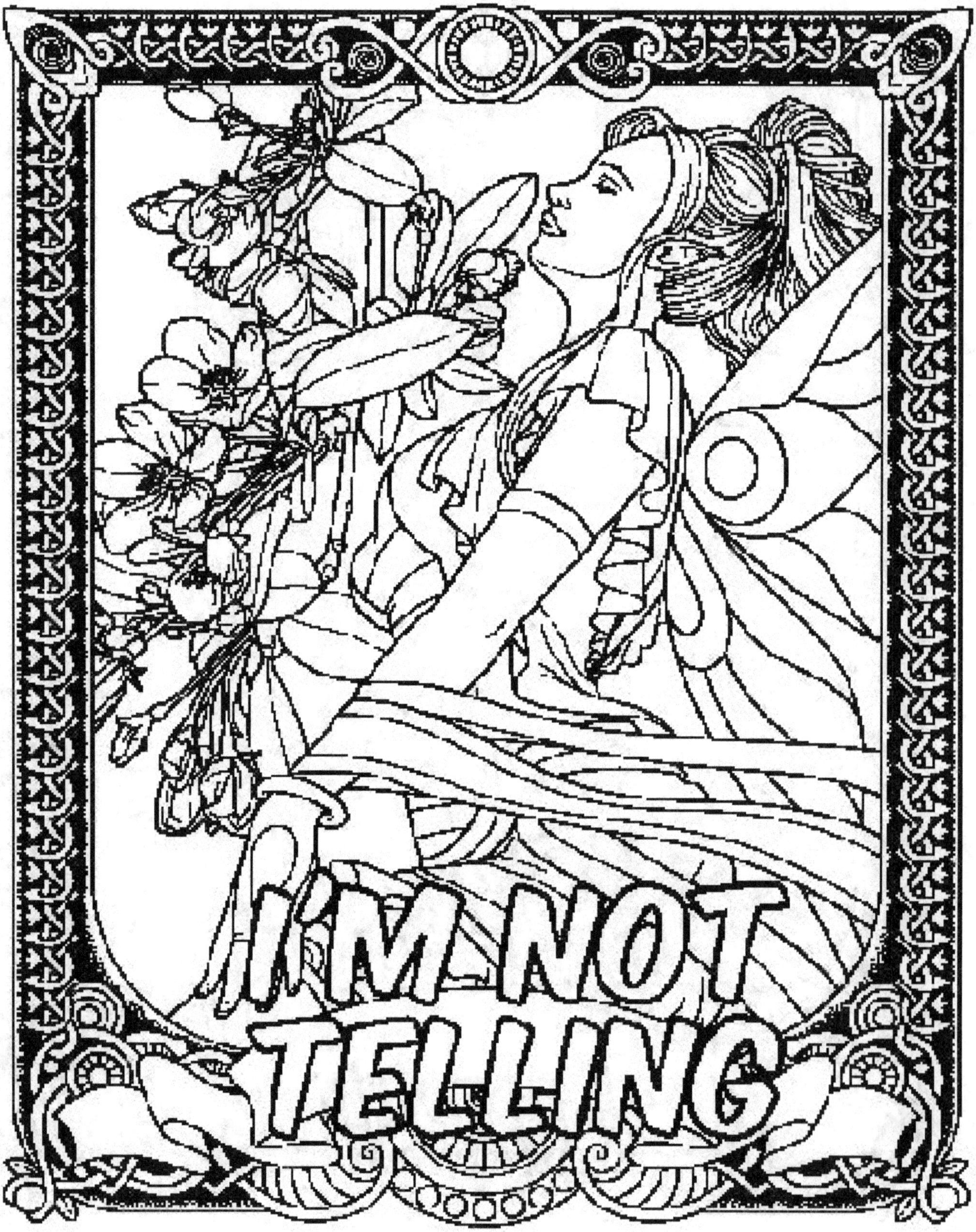
I'M NOT
TELLING

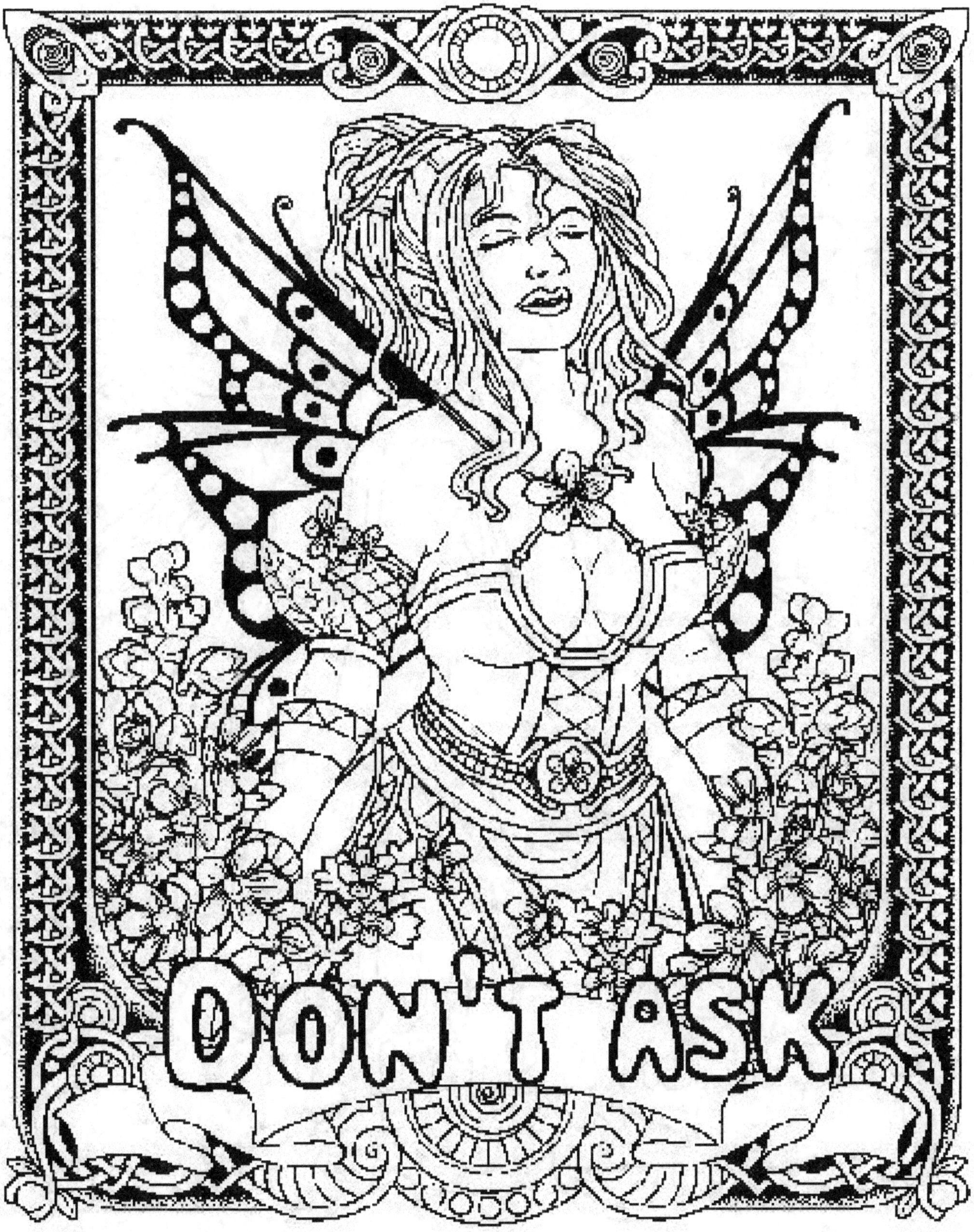
DON'T ASK

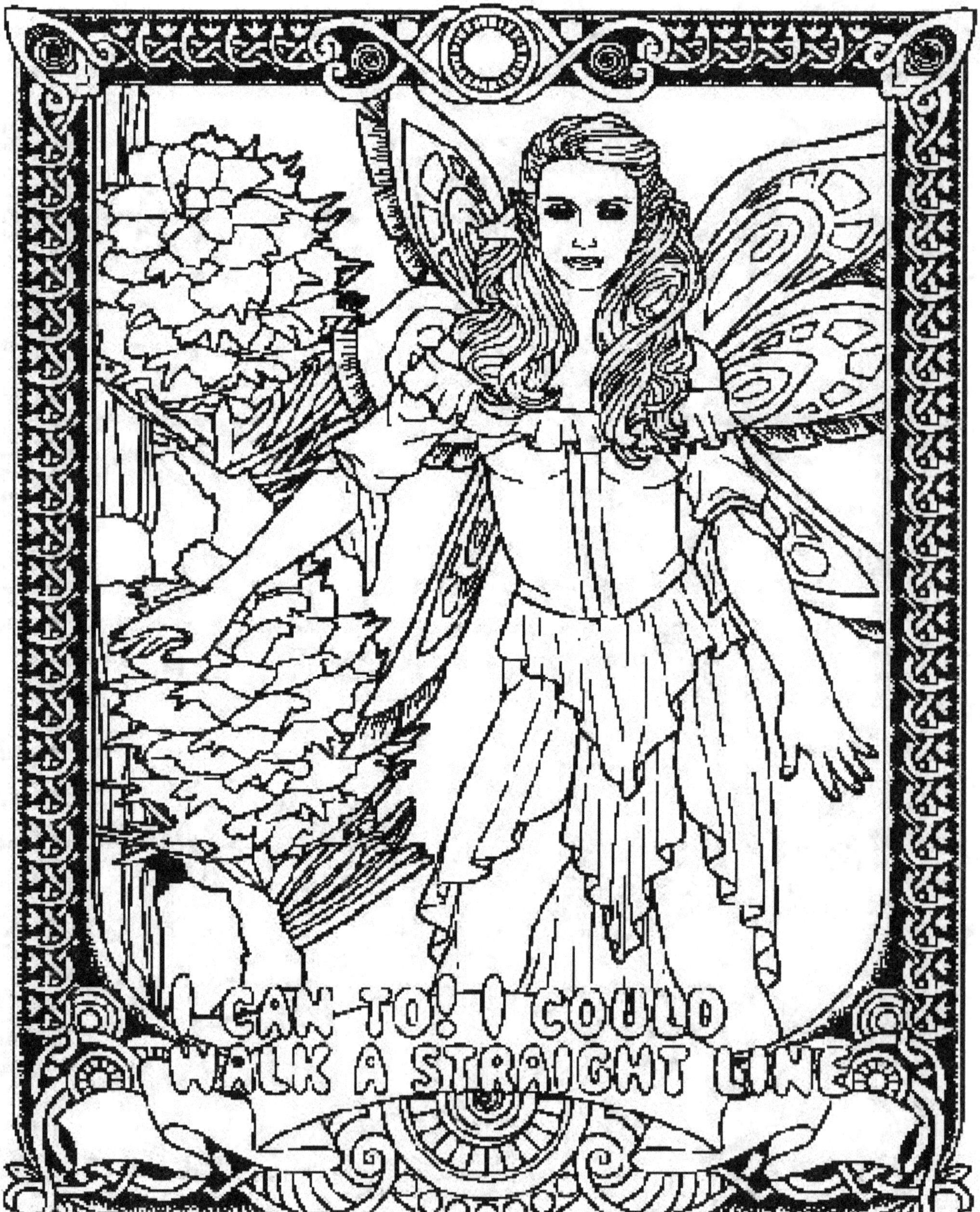
I CAN TO! I COULD
WALK A STRAIGHT LINE

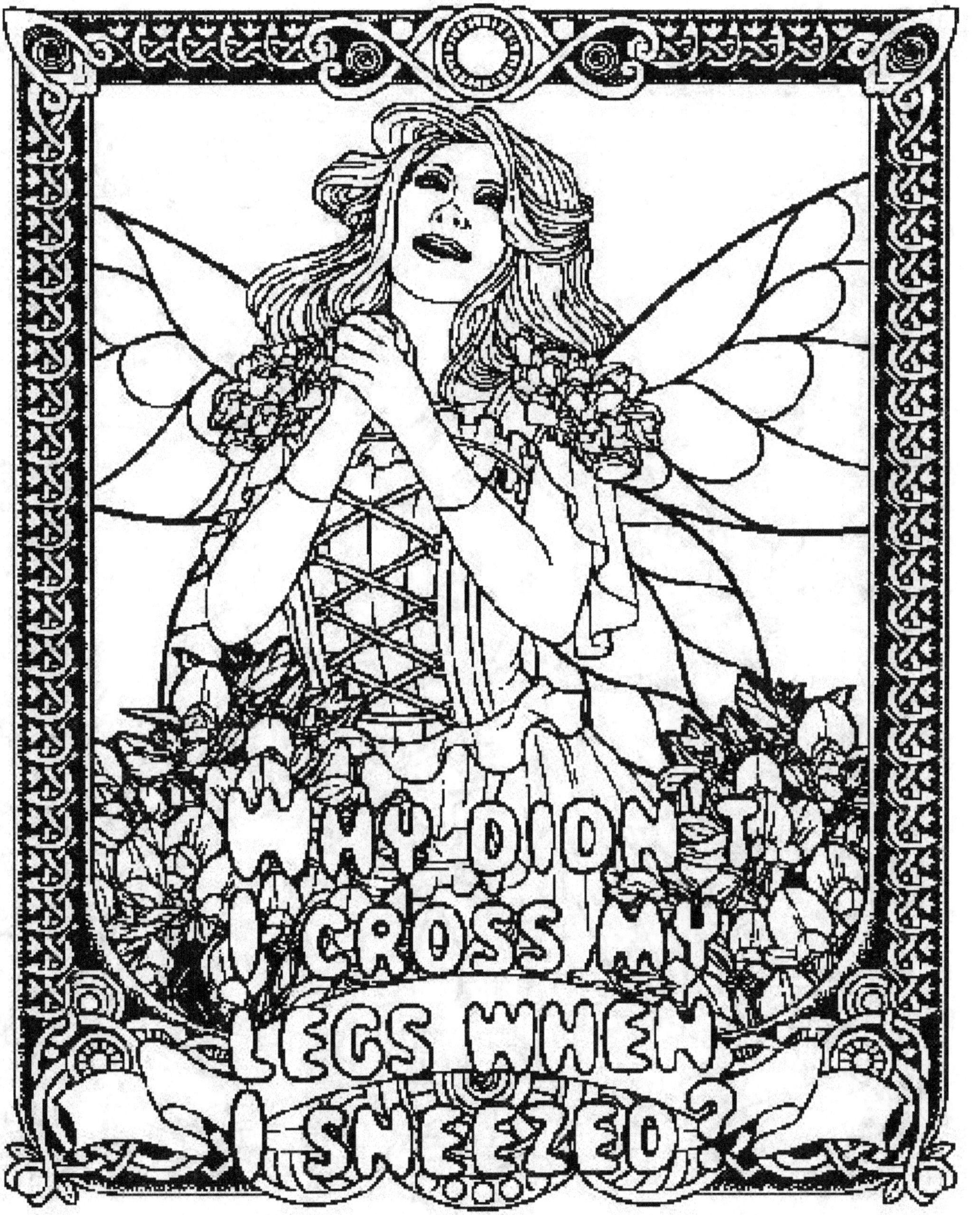
WHY DIDN'T
I CROSS MY
LEGS WHEN
I SNEEZED?

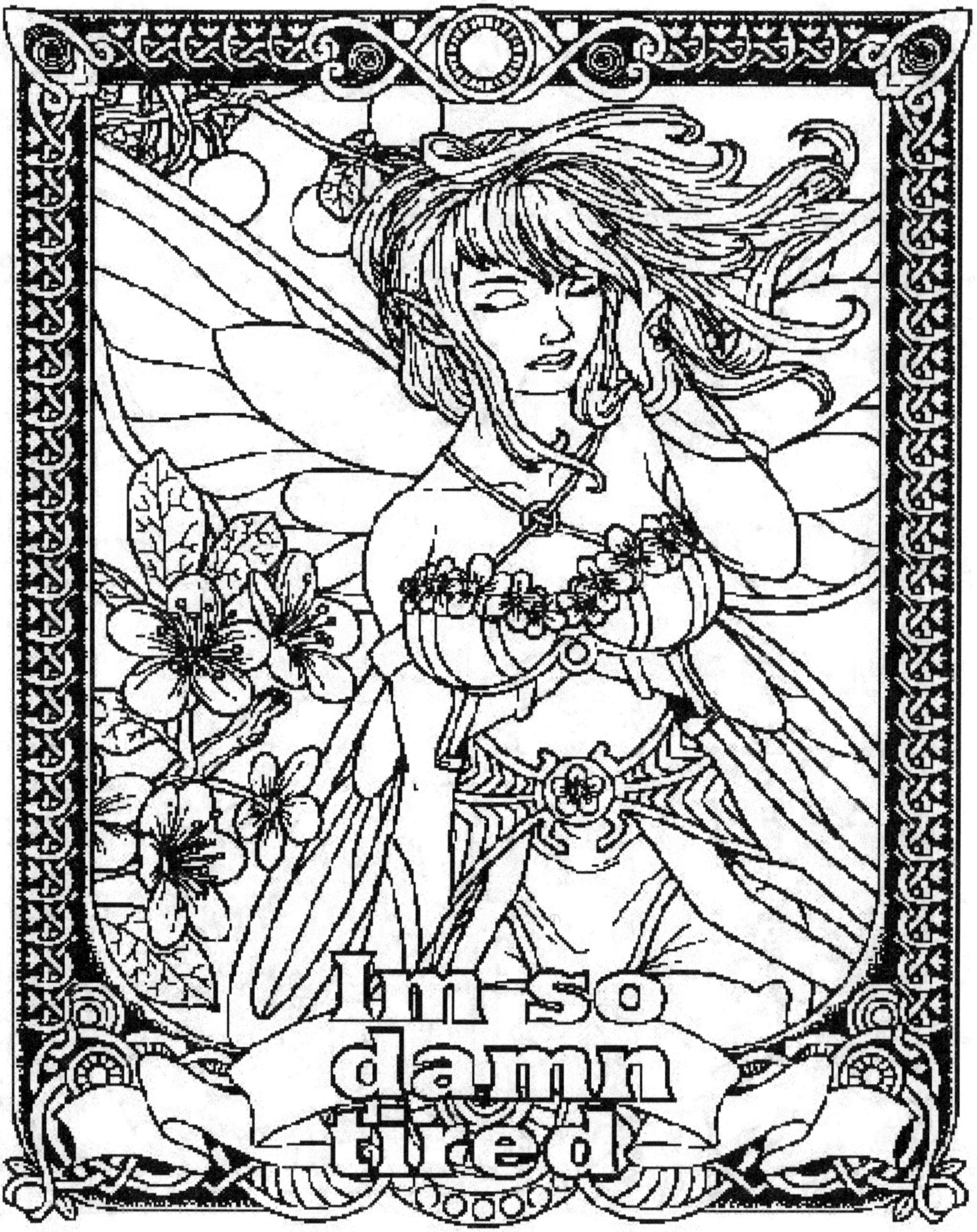
Im so
damn
tired

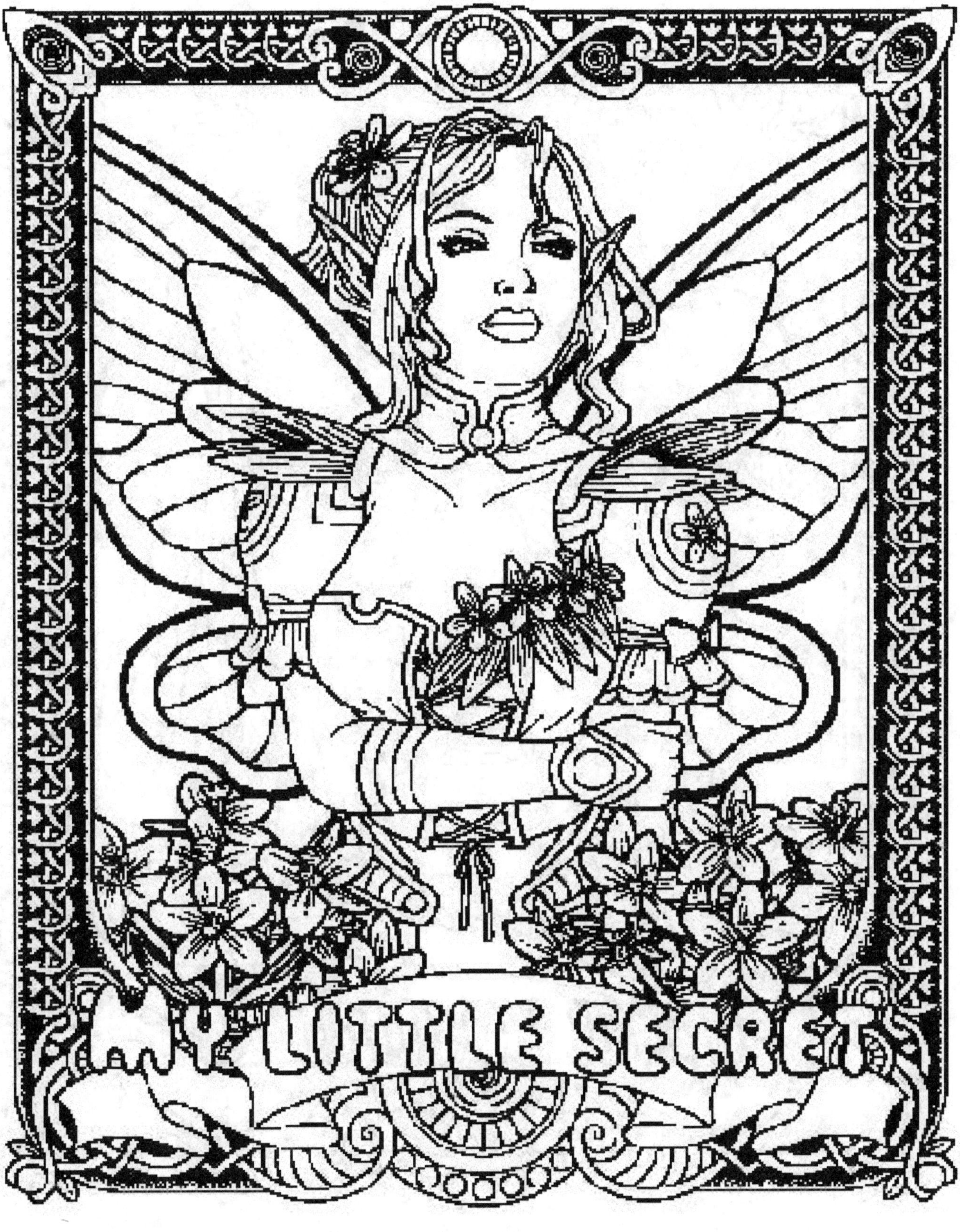
MY LITTLE SECRET

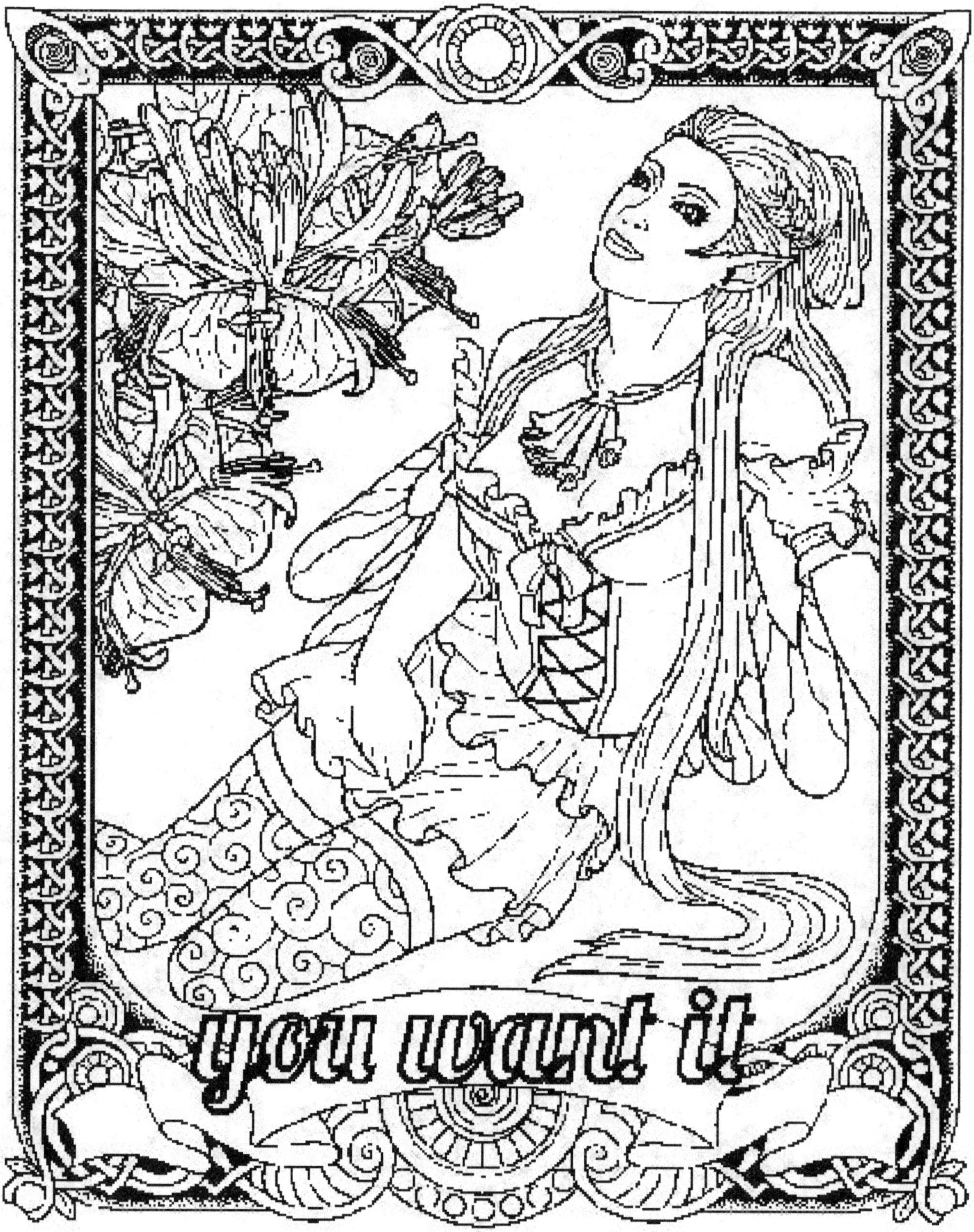
you want it

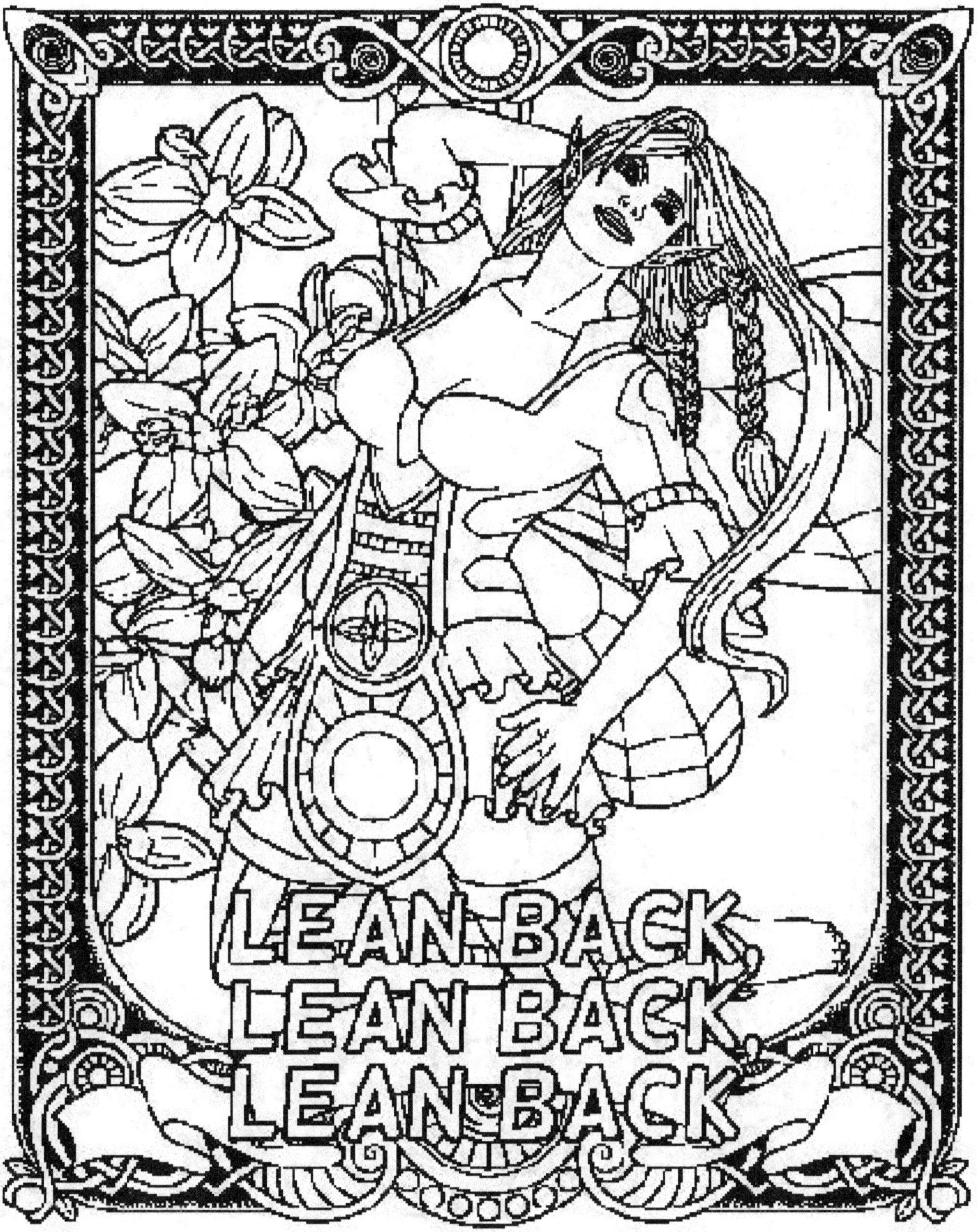
LEAN BACK,
LEAN BACK,
LEAN BACK

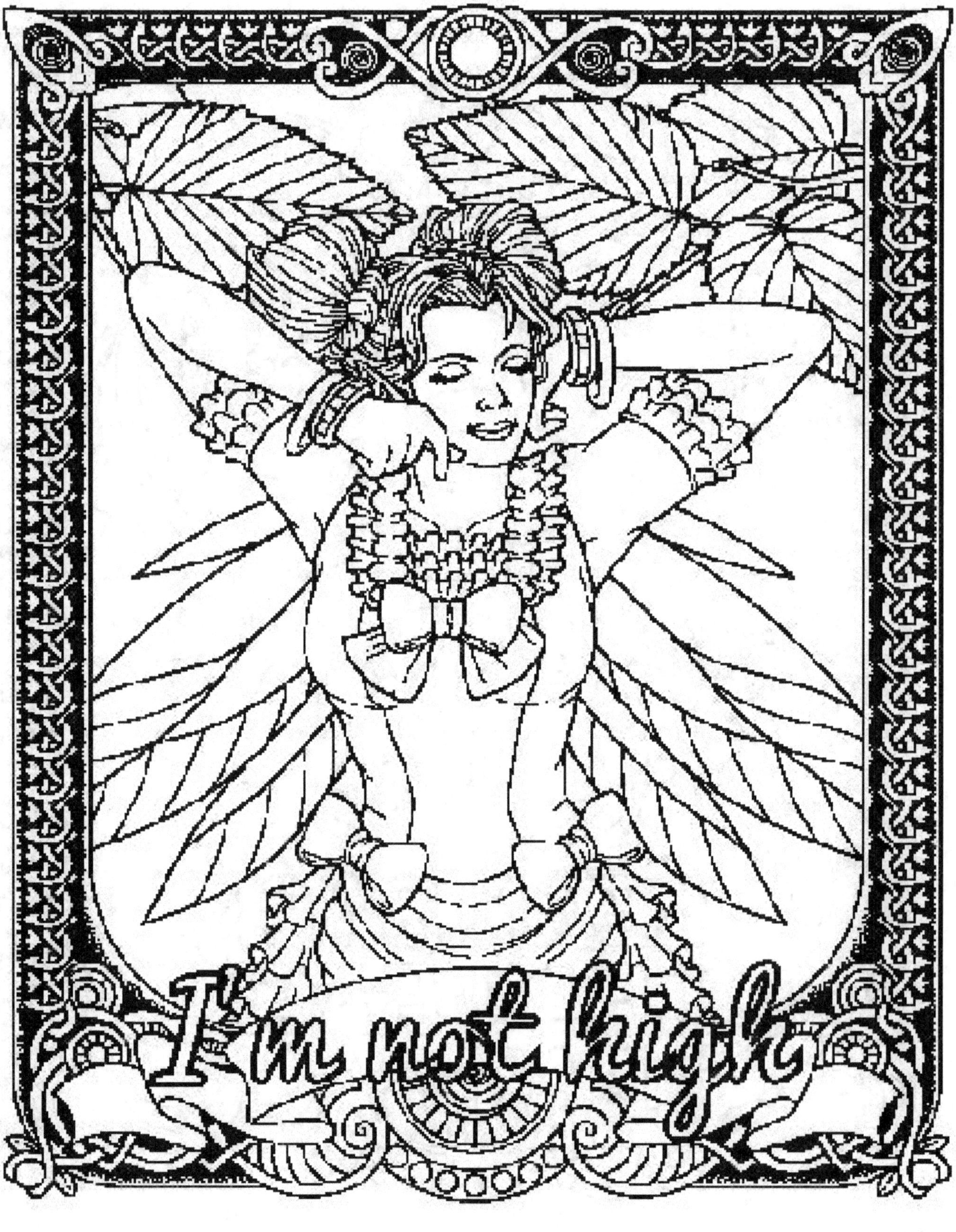
I'm not high

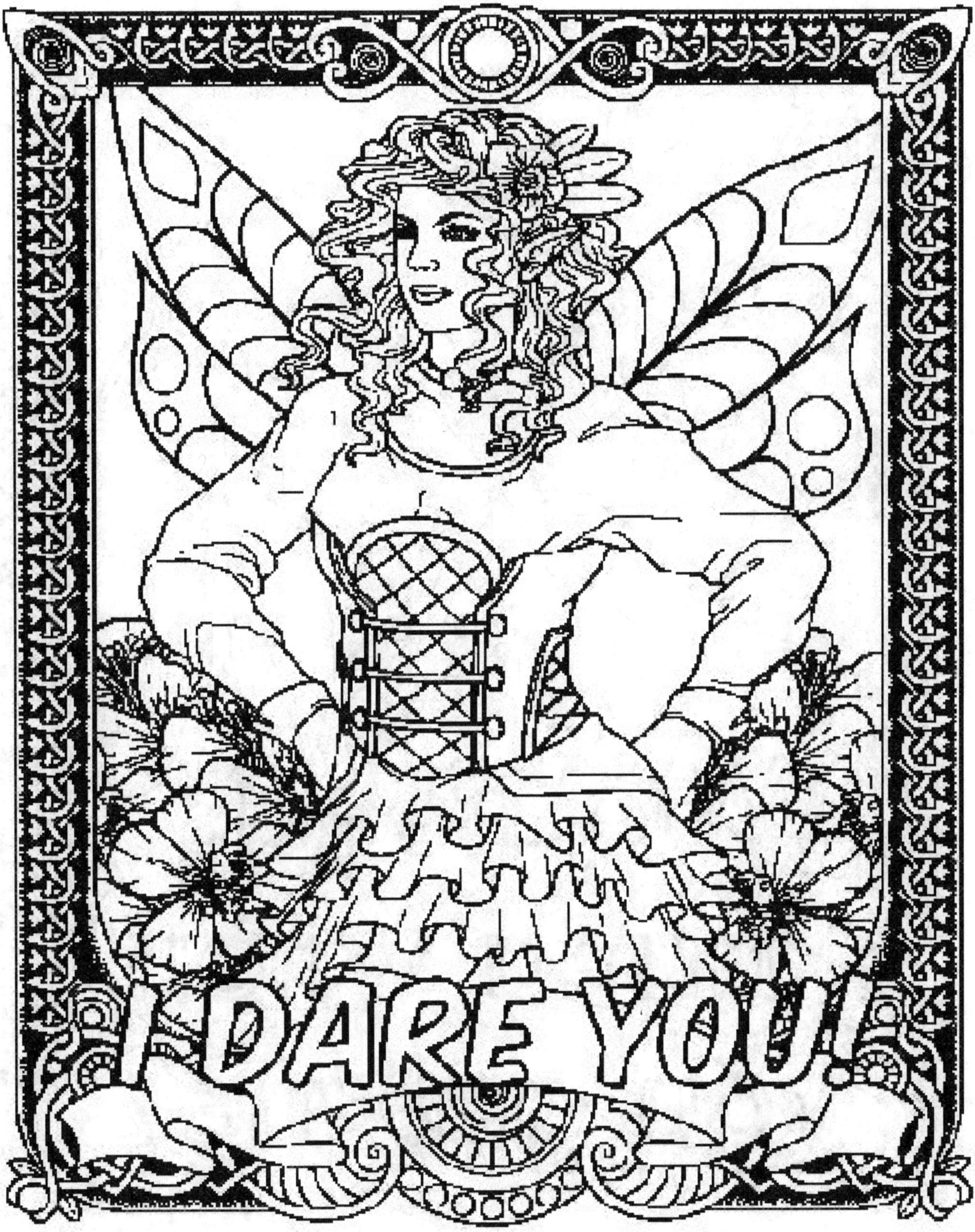
I DARE YOU!

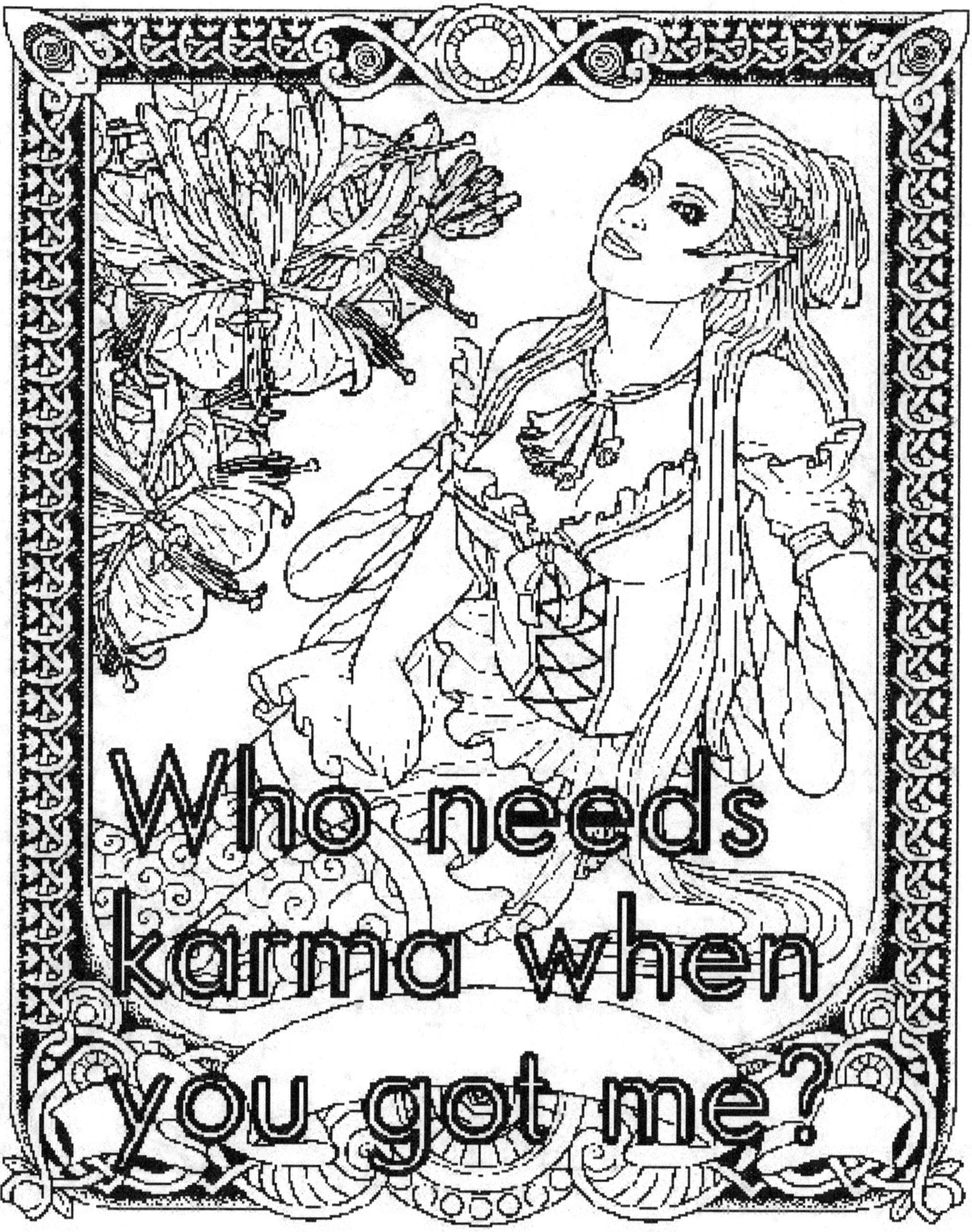
Who needs
karma when
you got me?

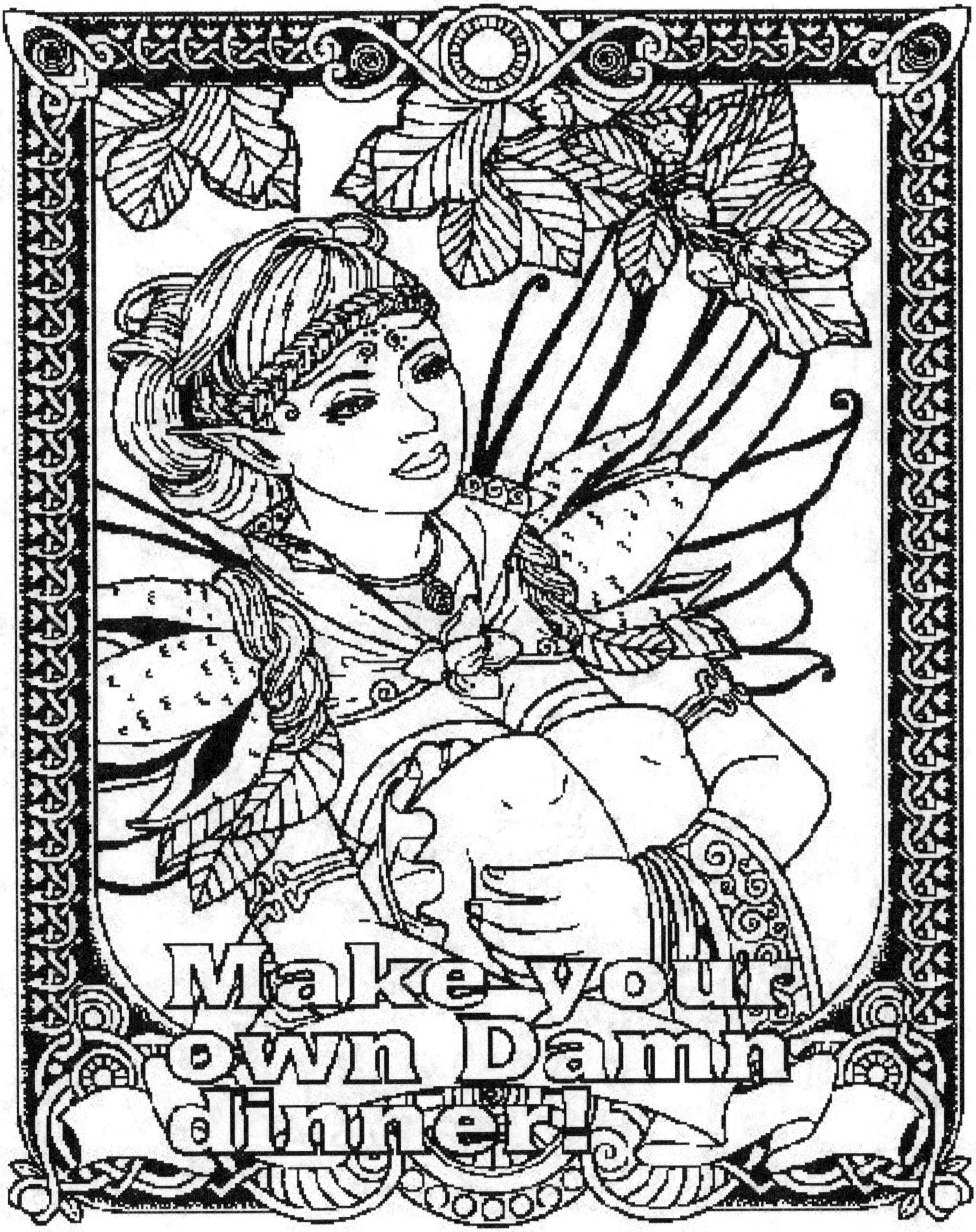
Make your
own Damn
dinner!

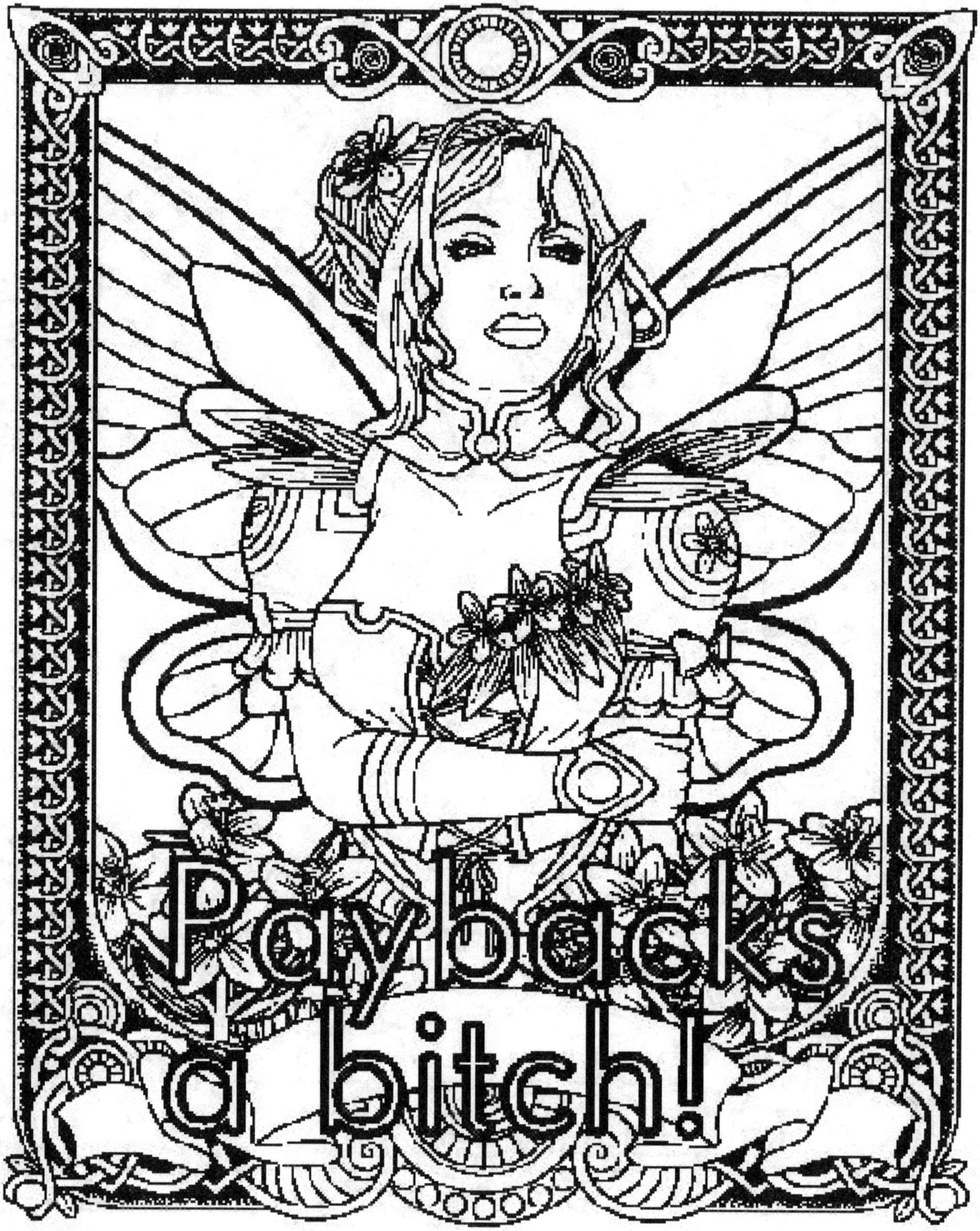
Paybacks
a bitch!

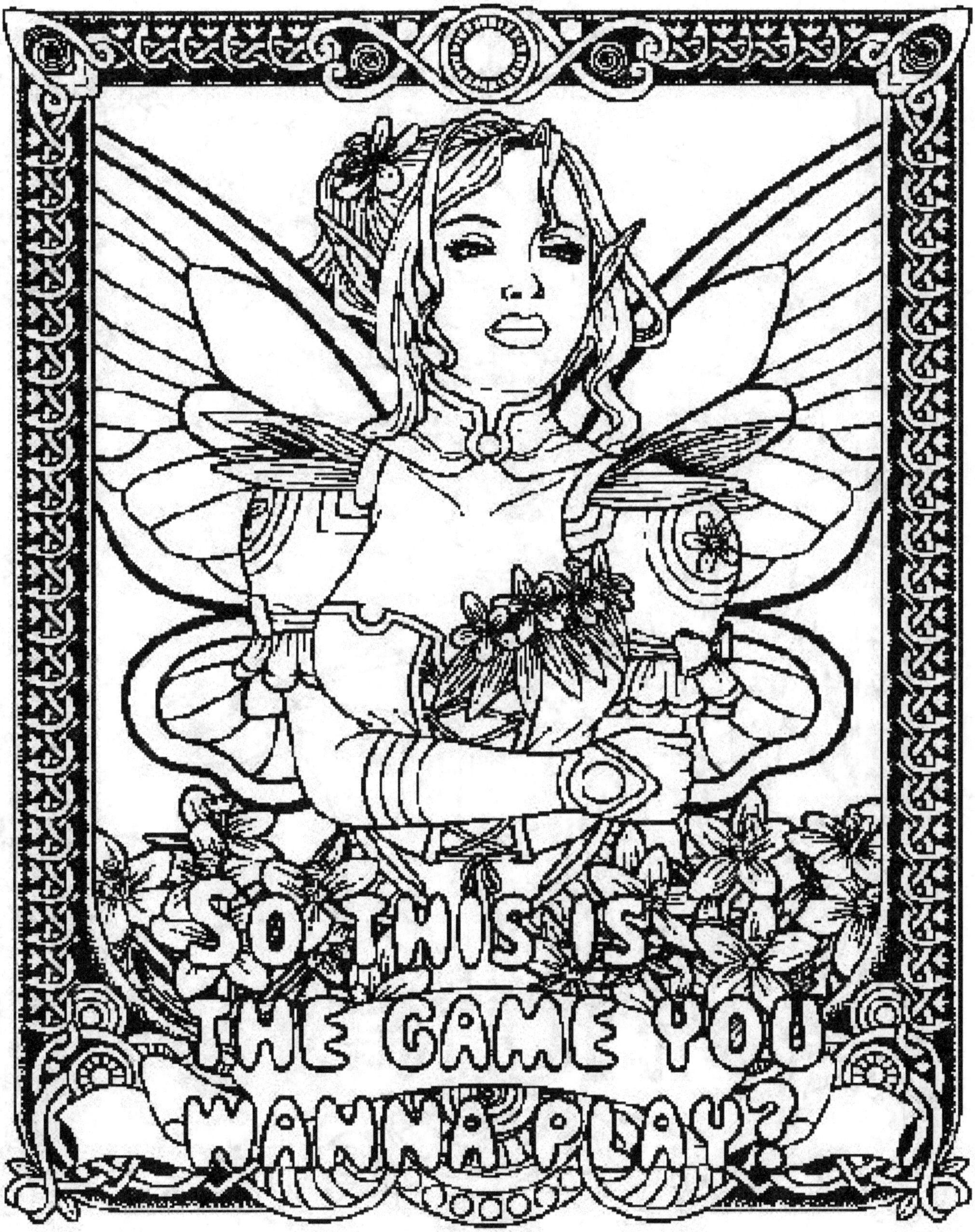
SO THIS IS
THE GAME YOU
WANNA PLAY?

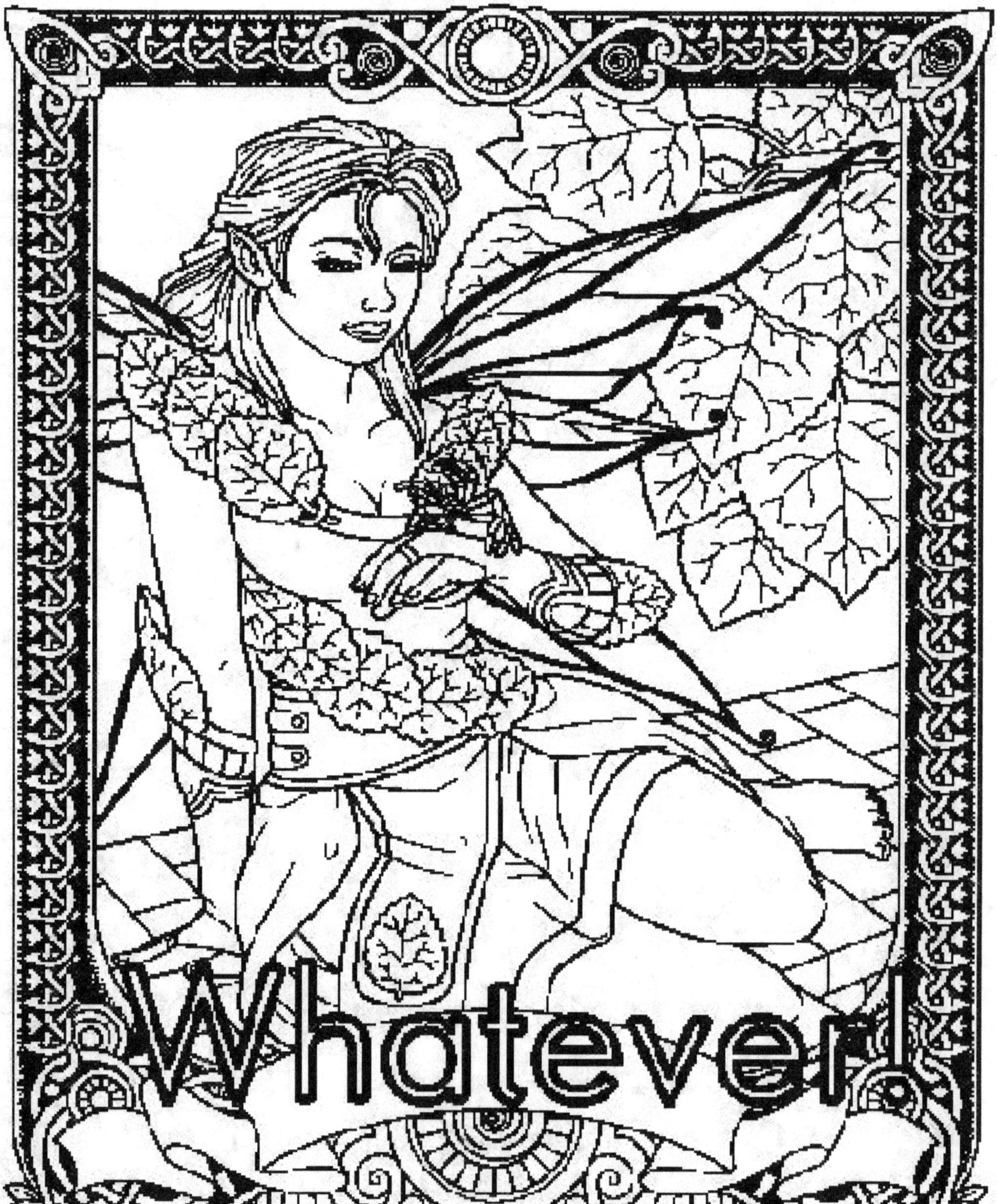
Whatever!

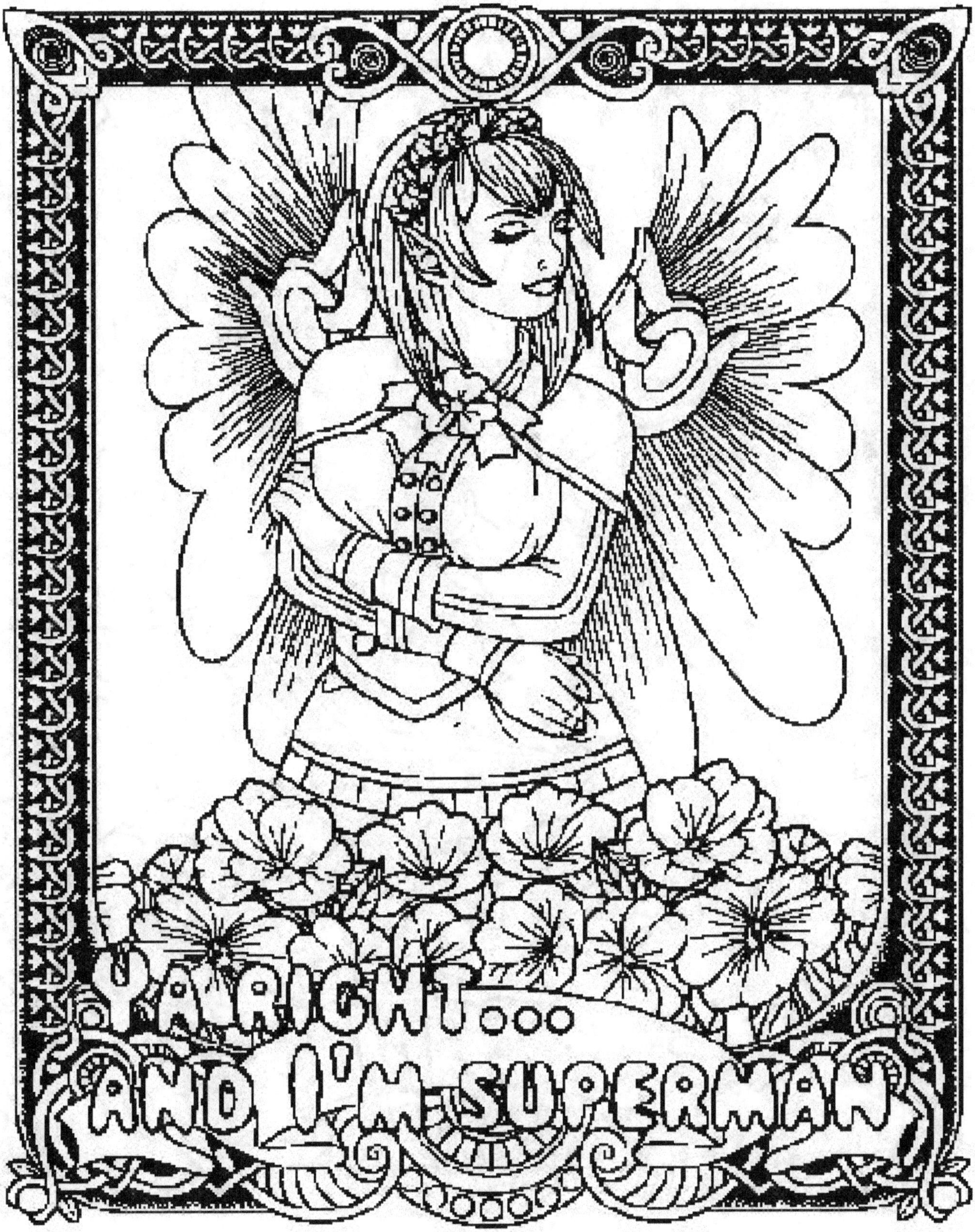
YA RIGHT...
AND I'M SUPERMAN

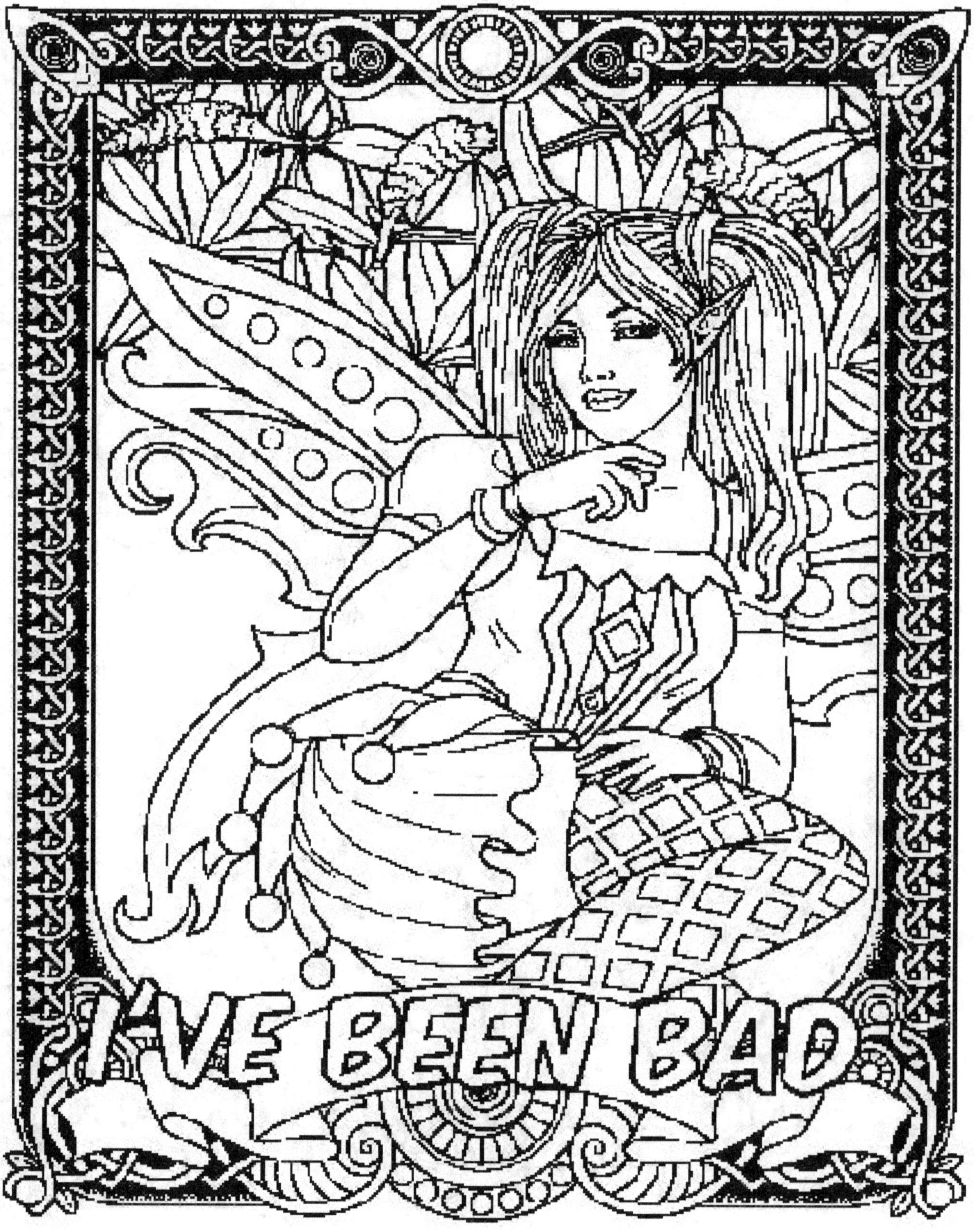
I'VE BEEN BAD

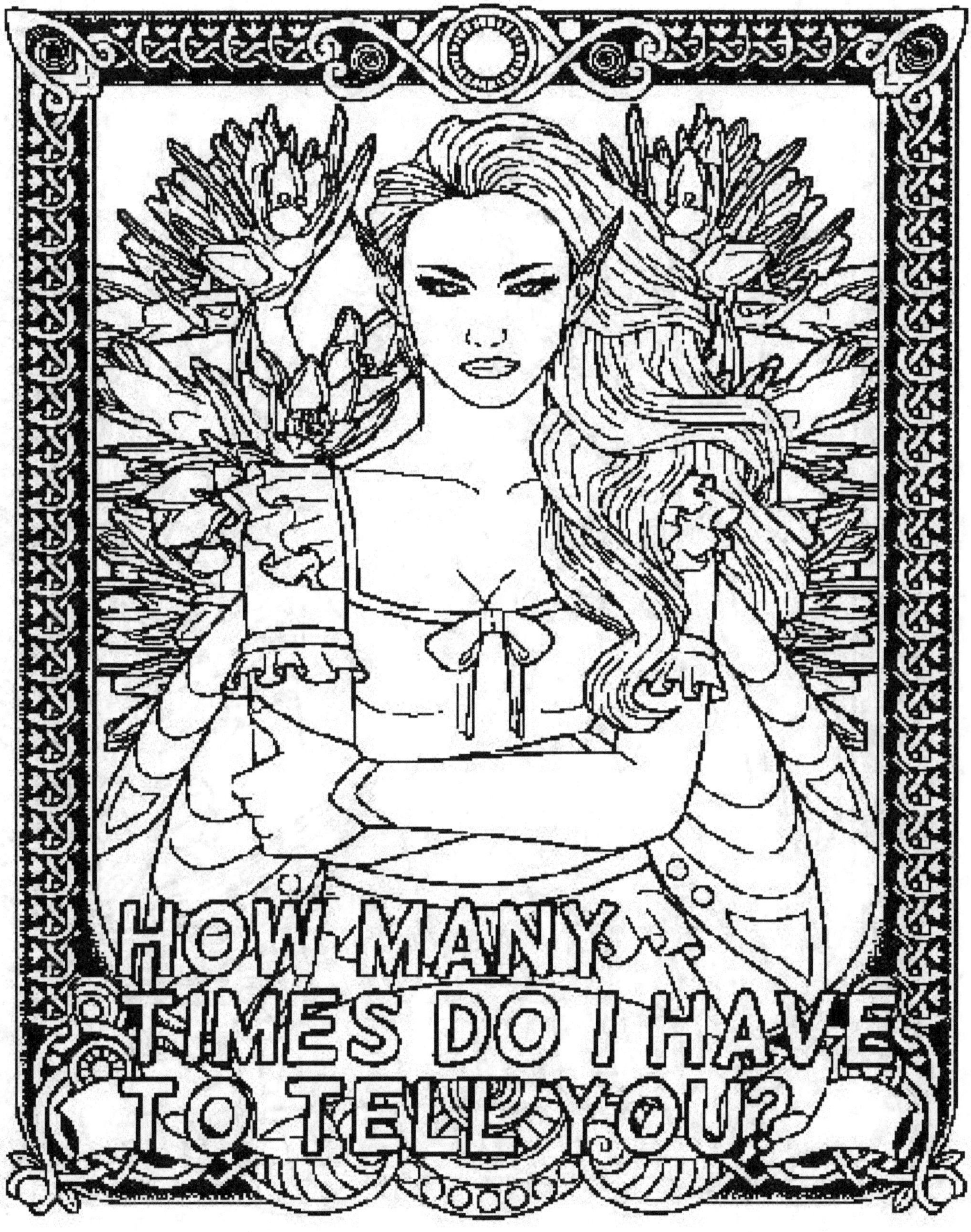
HOW MANY
TIMES DO I HAVE
TO TELL YOU?

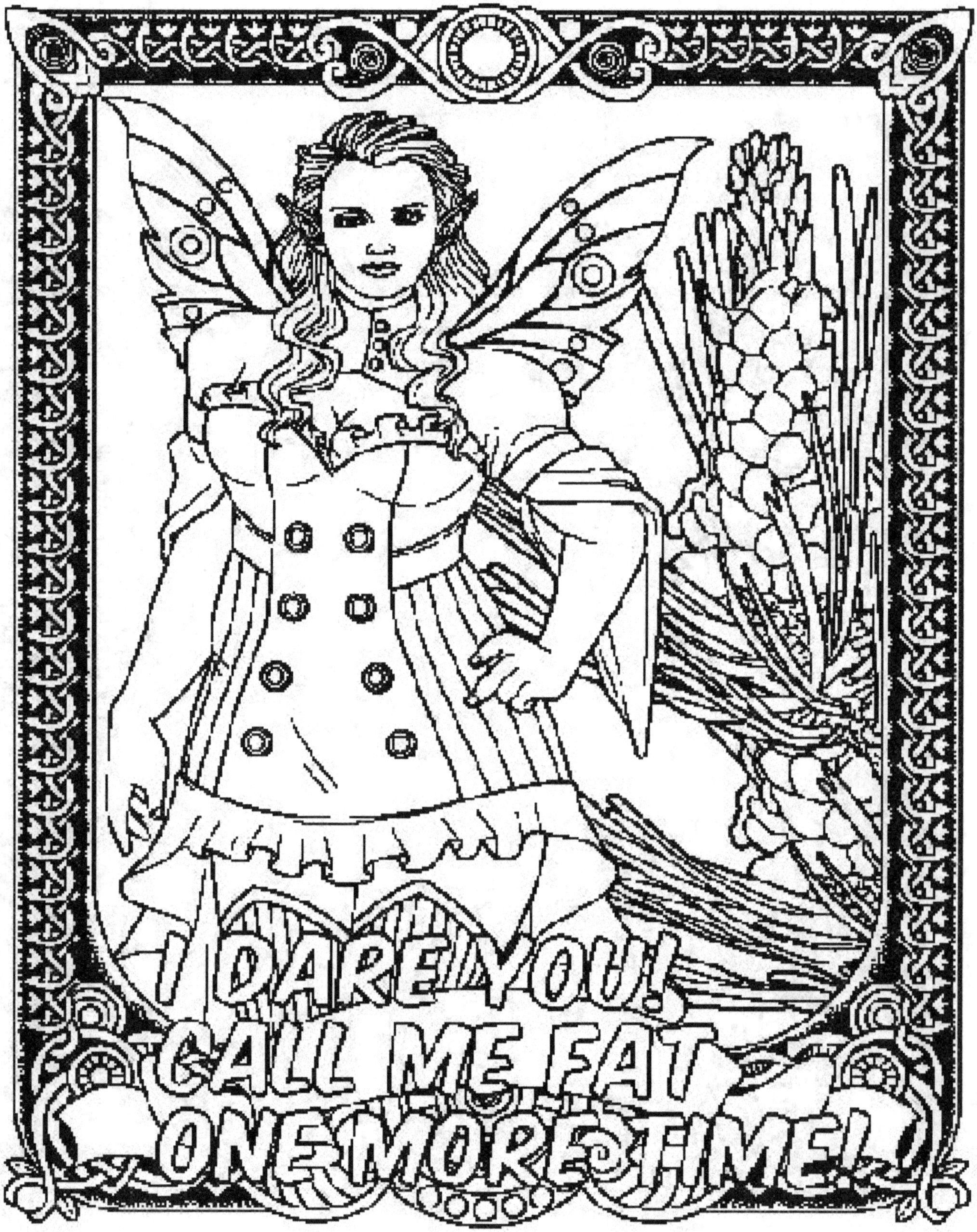
I DARE YOU!
CALL ME FAT
ONE MORE TIME!

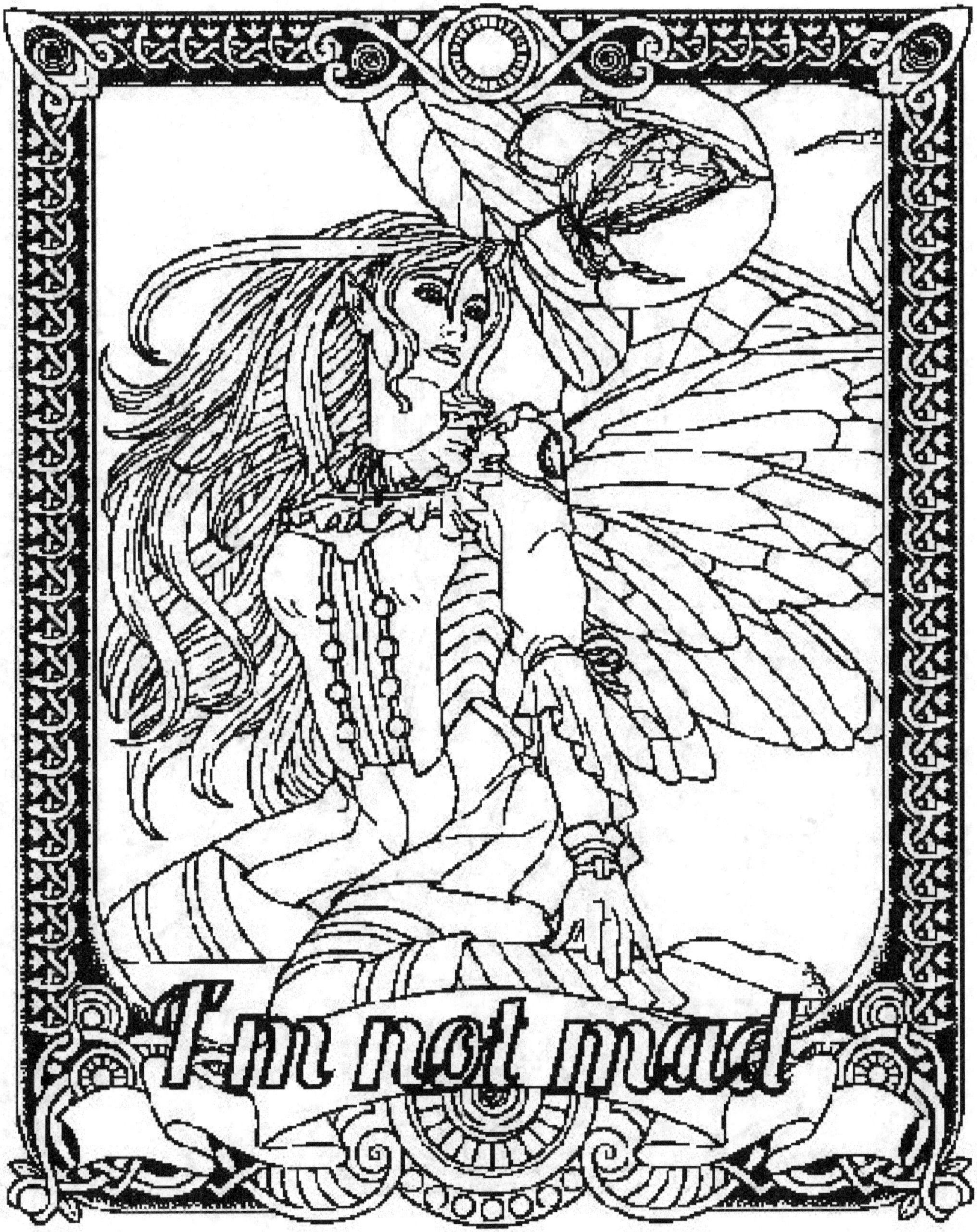
I'm not mad

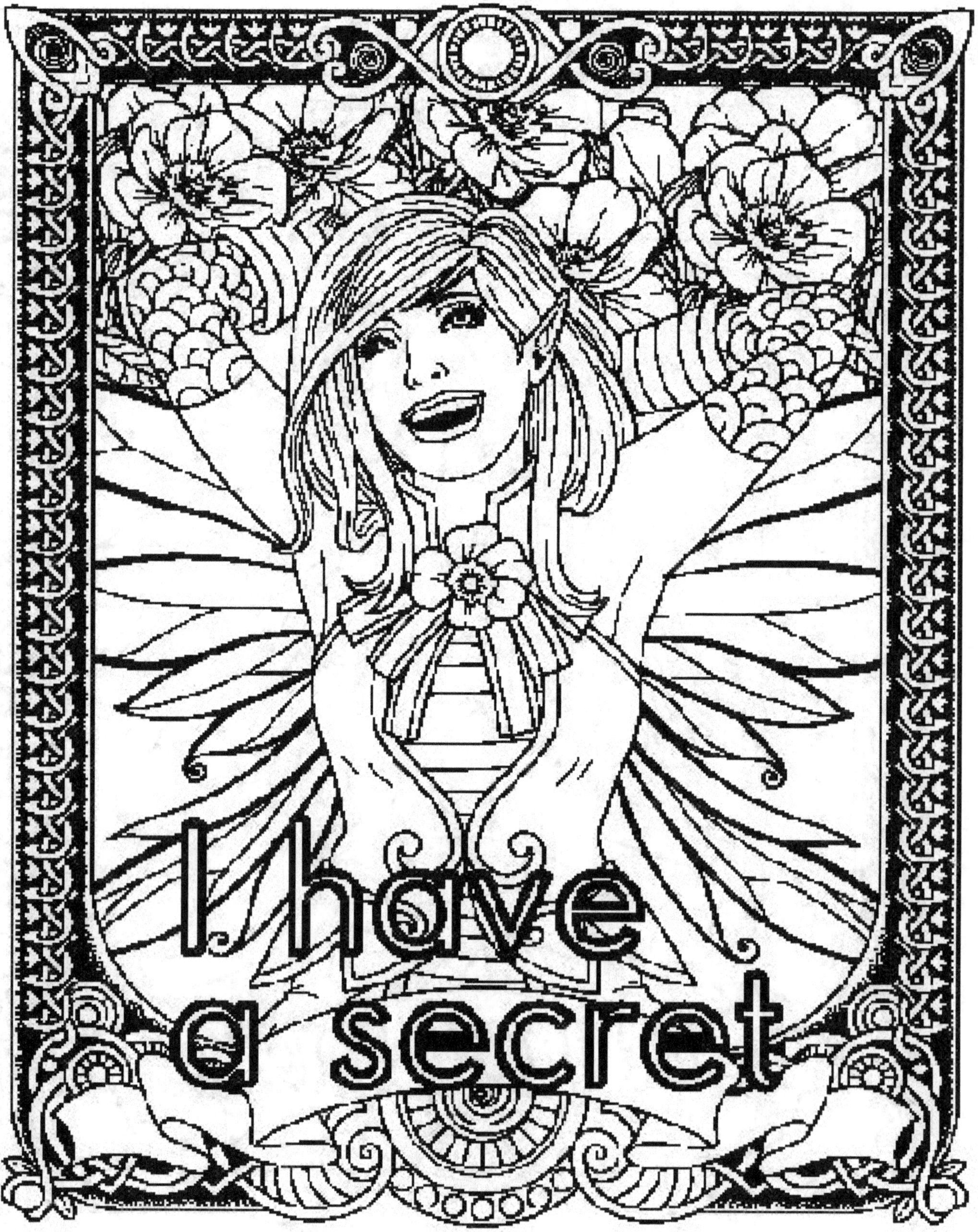
I have
a secret

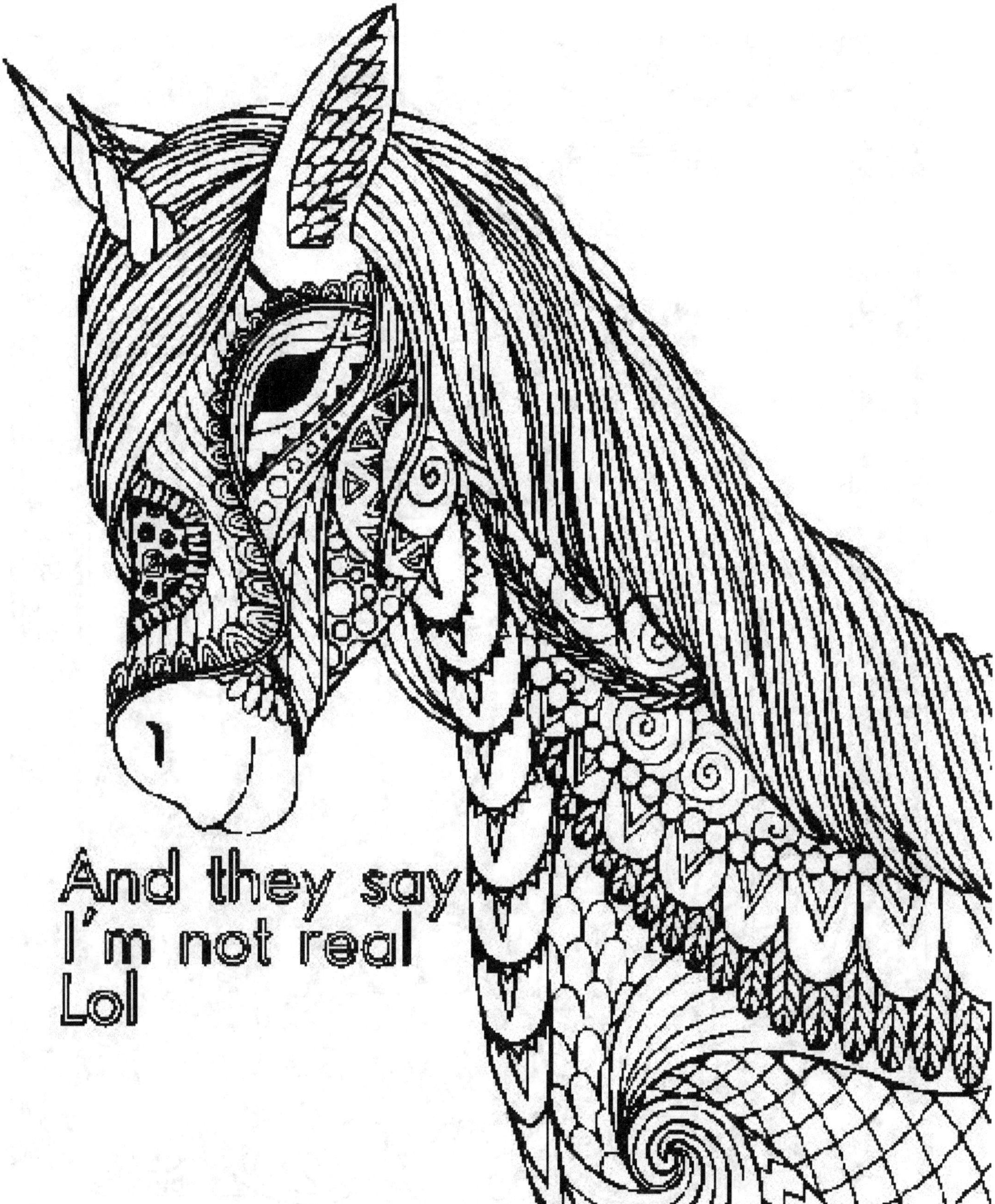
And they say
I'm not real
Lol

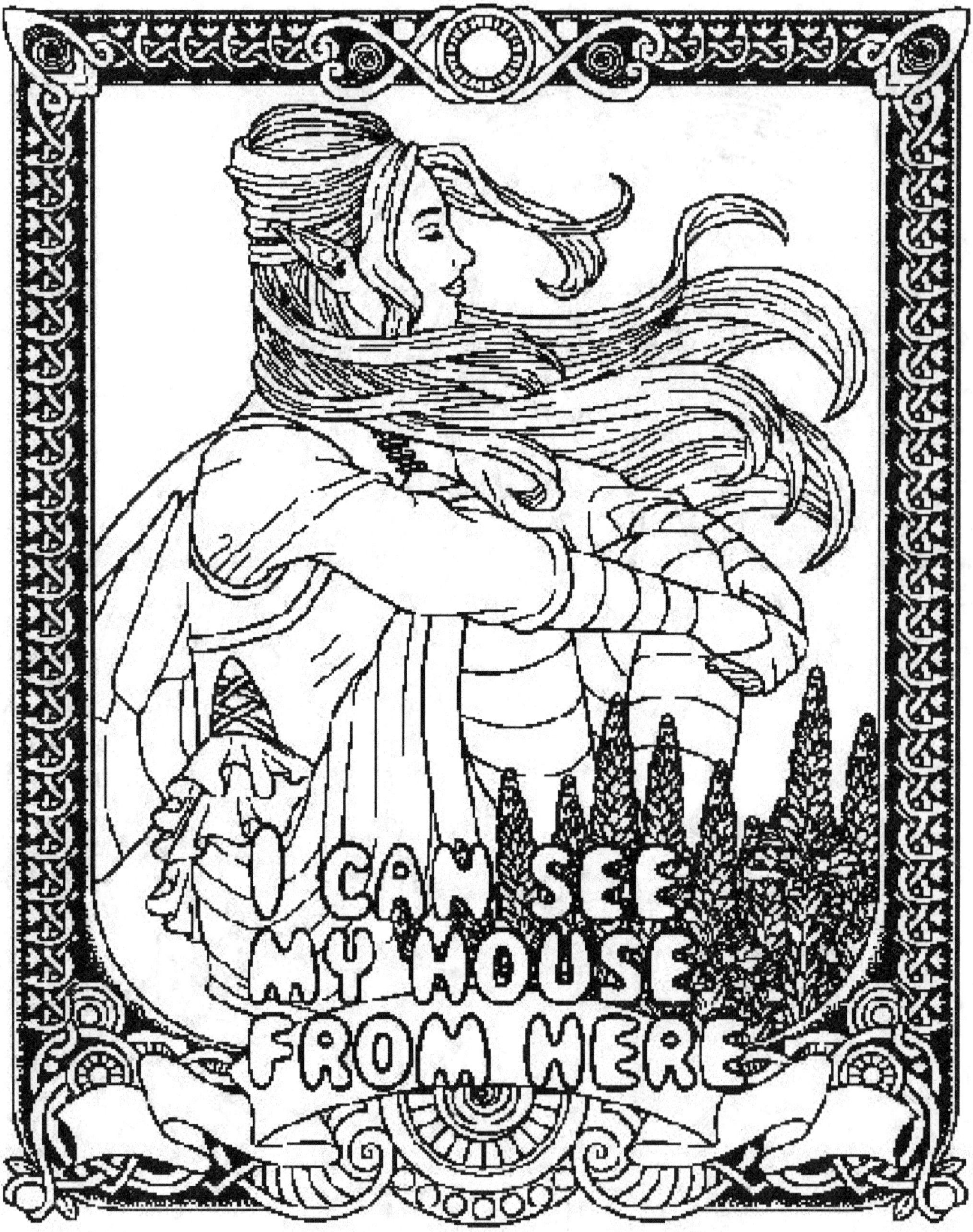
I CAN SEE
MY HOUSE
FROM HERE

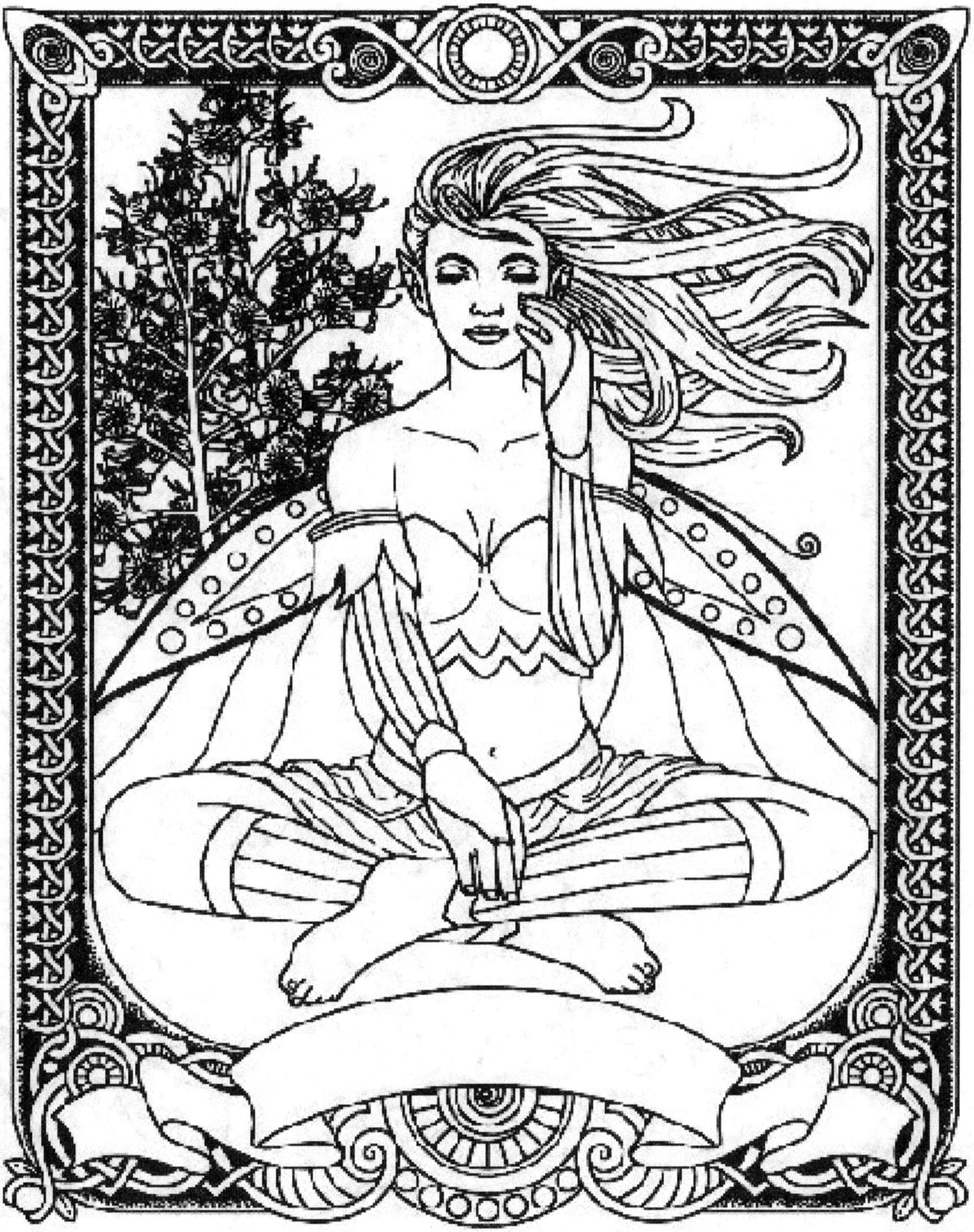

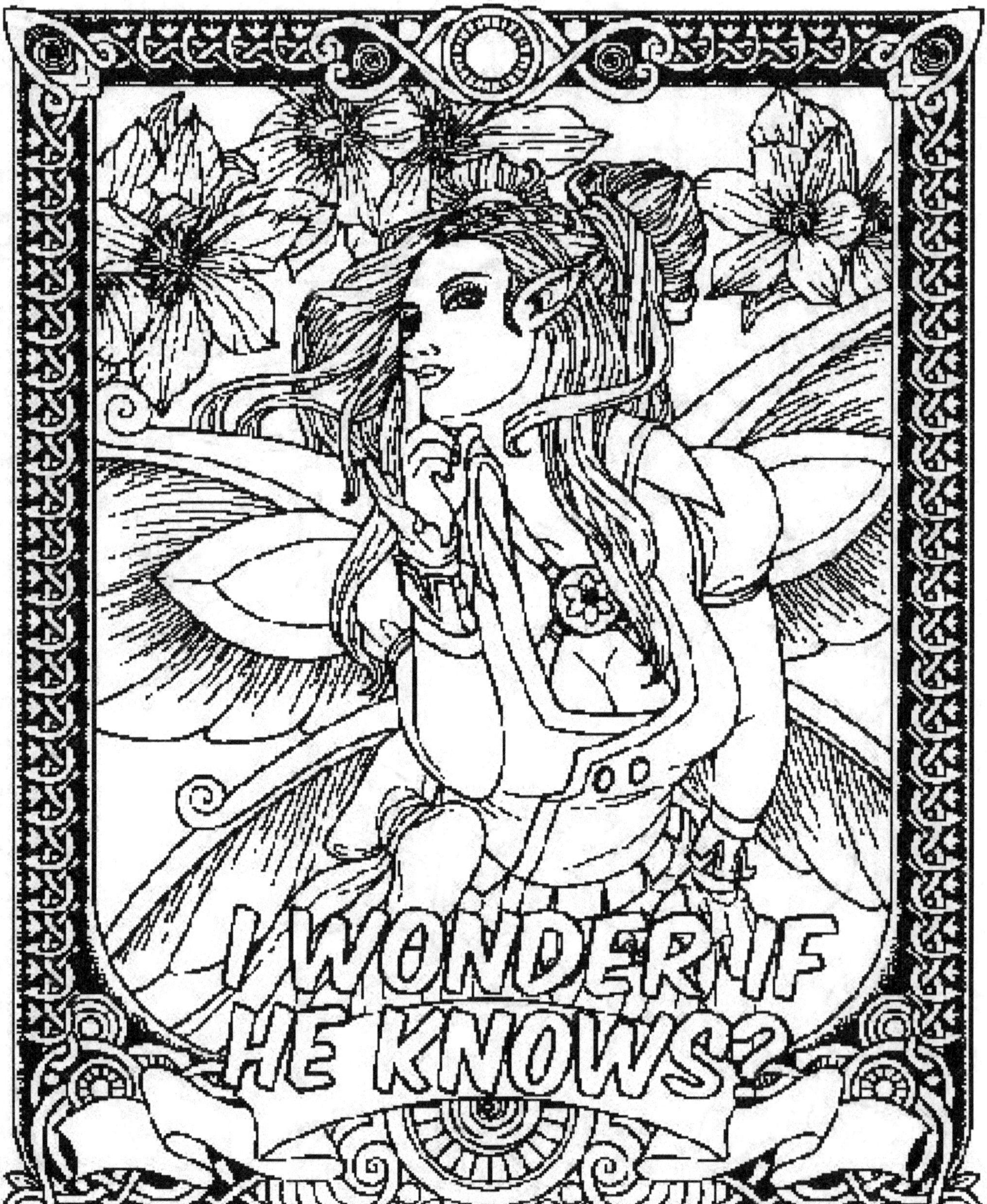
I WONDER IF
HE KNOWS?

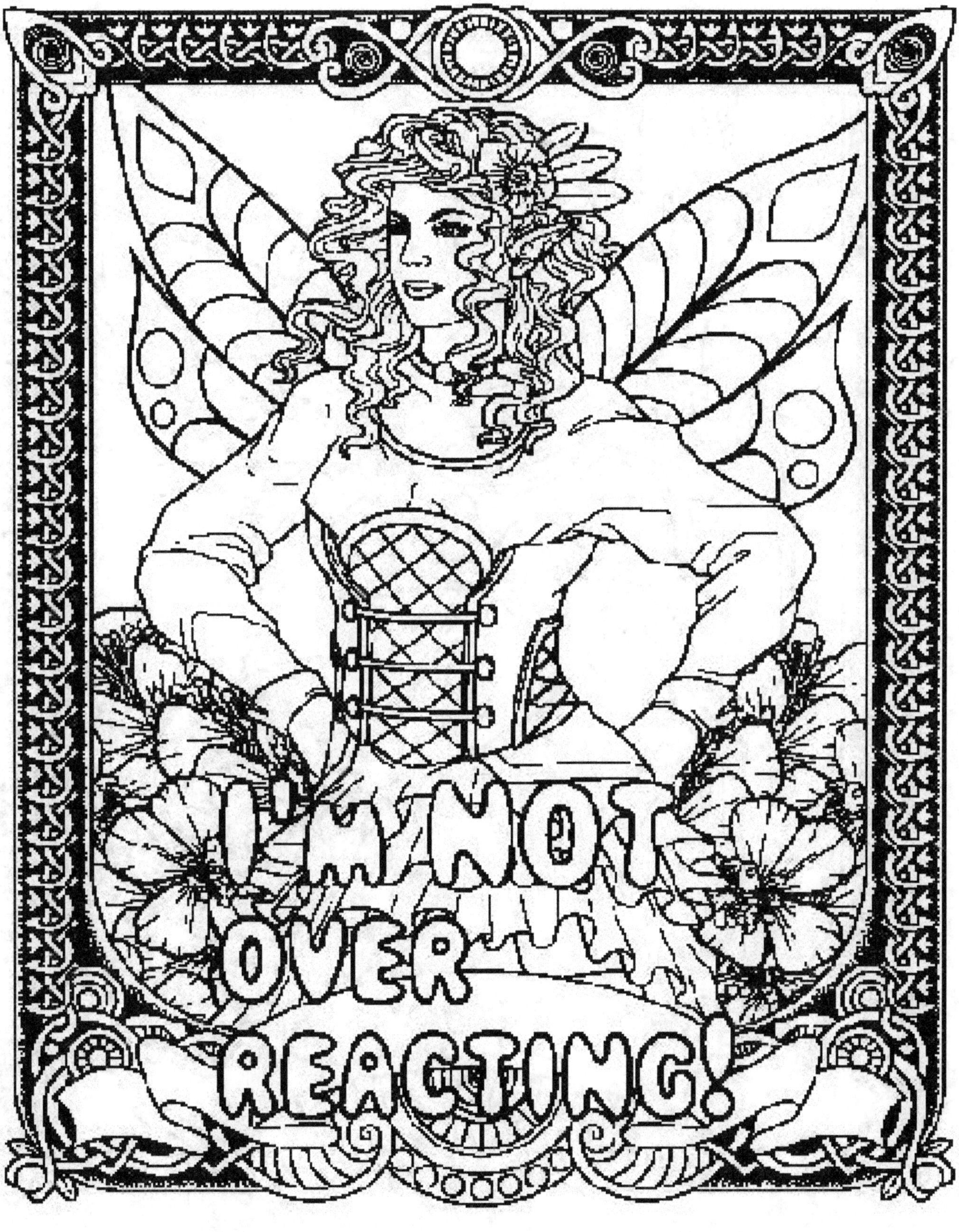
I'M NOT
OVER
REACTING!

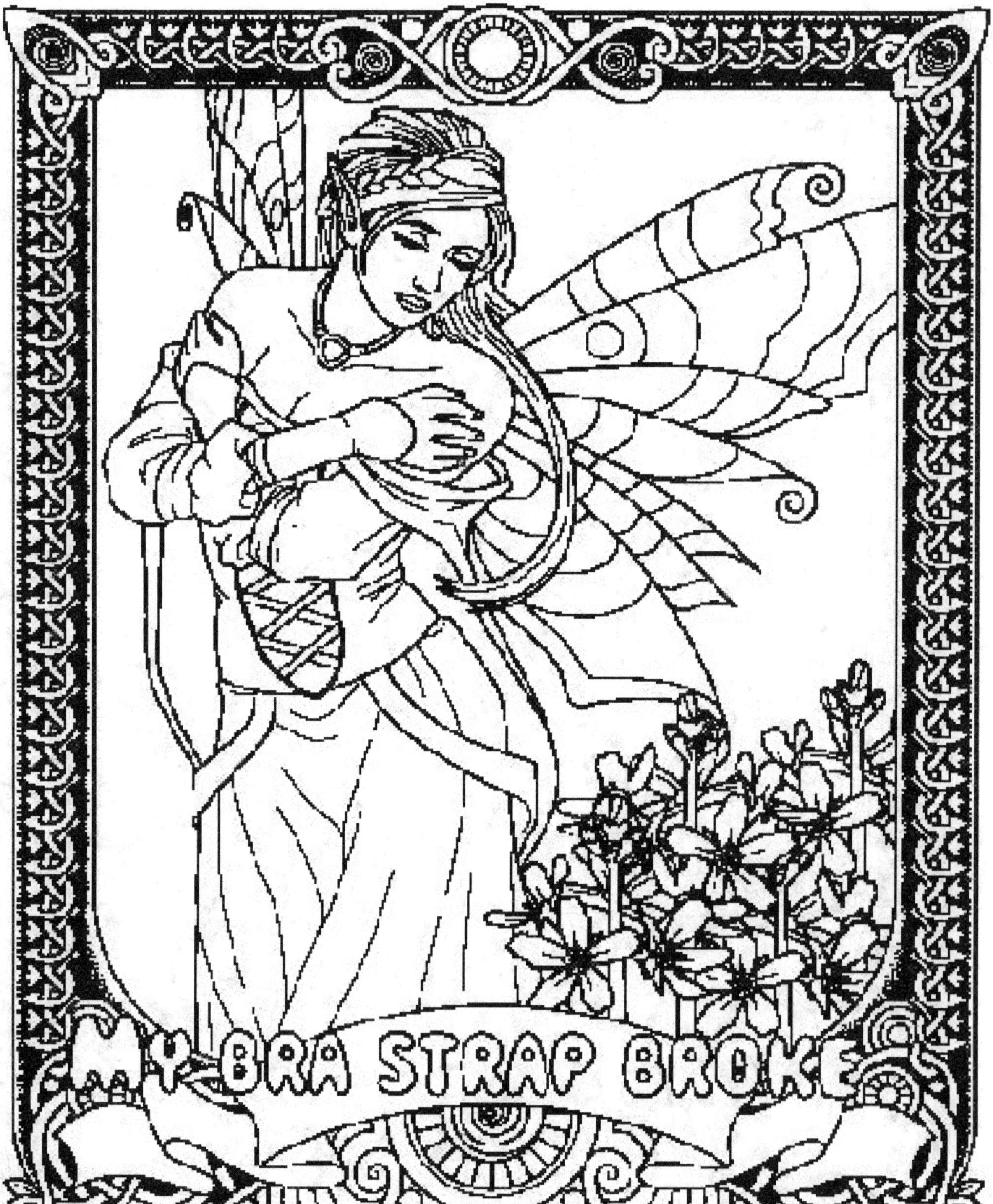
MY BRA STRAP BROKE

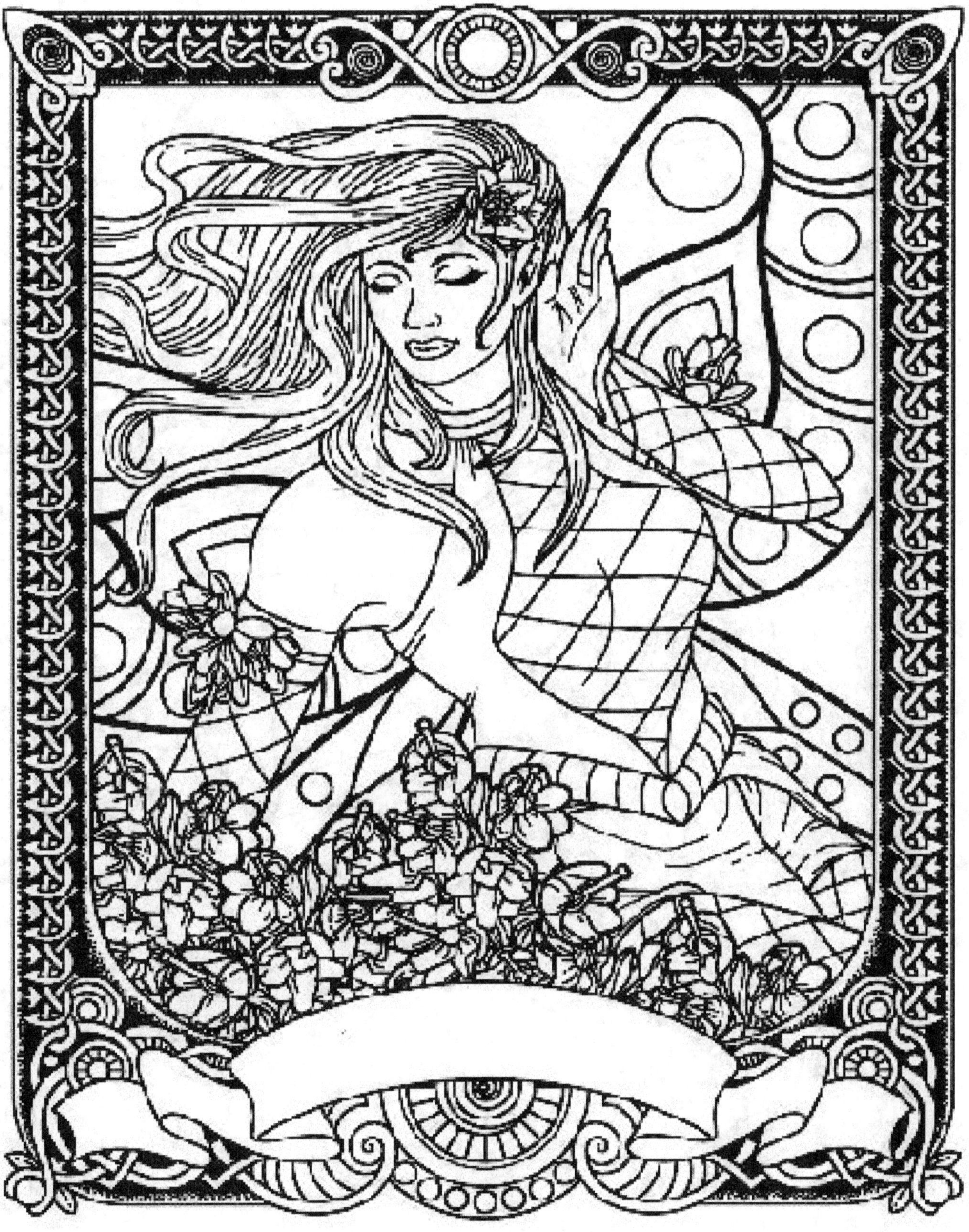

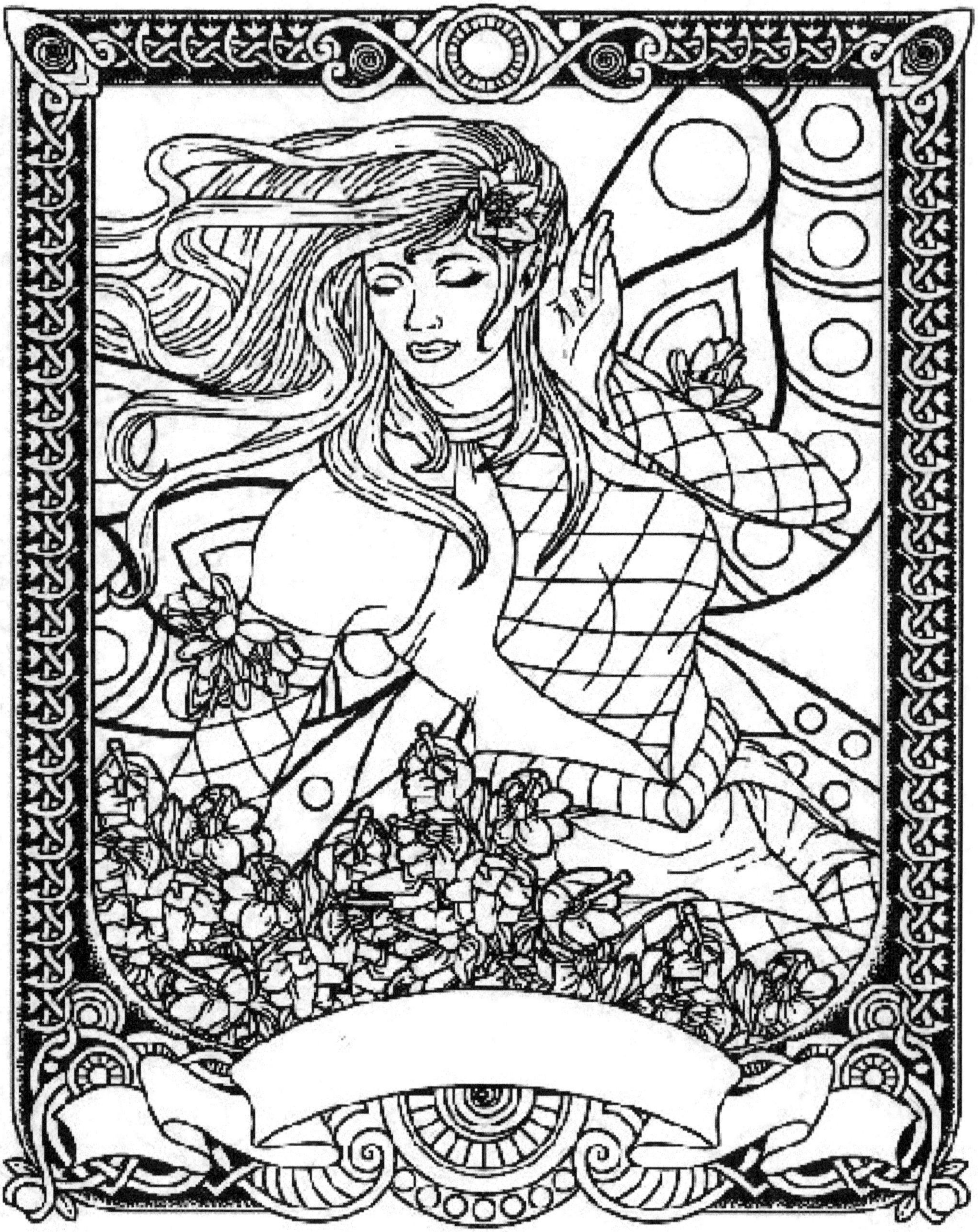

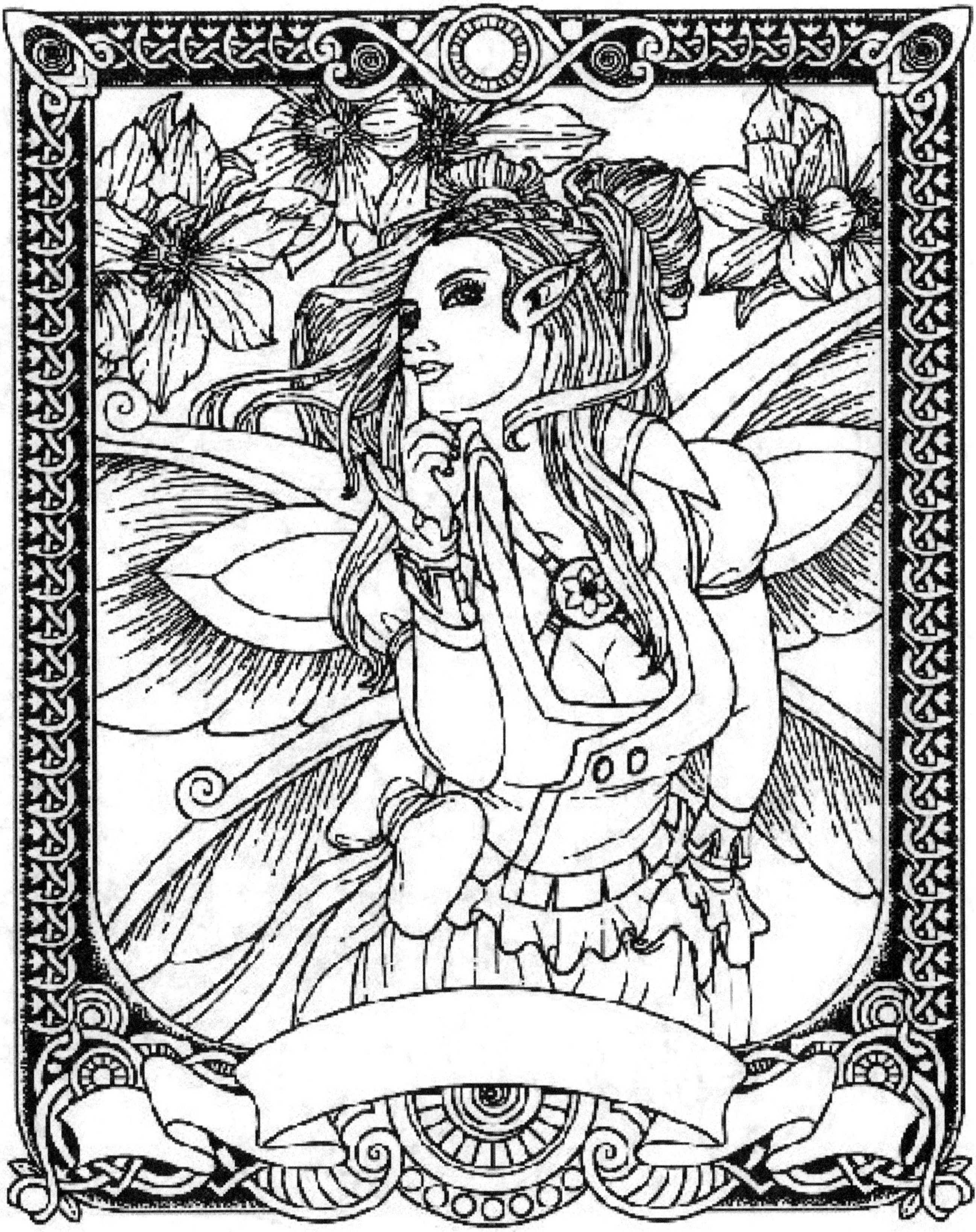

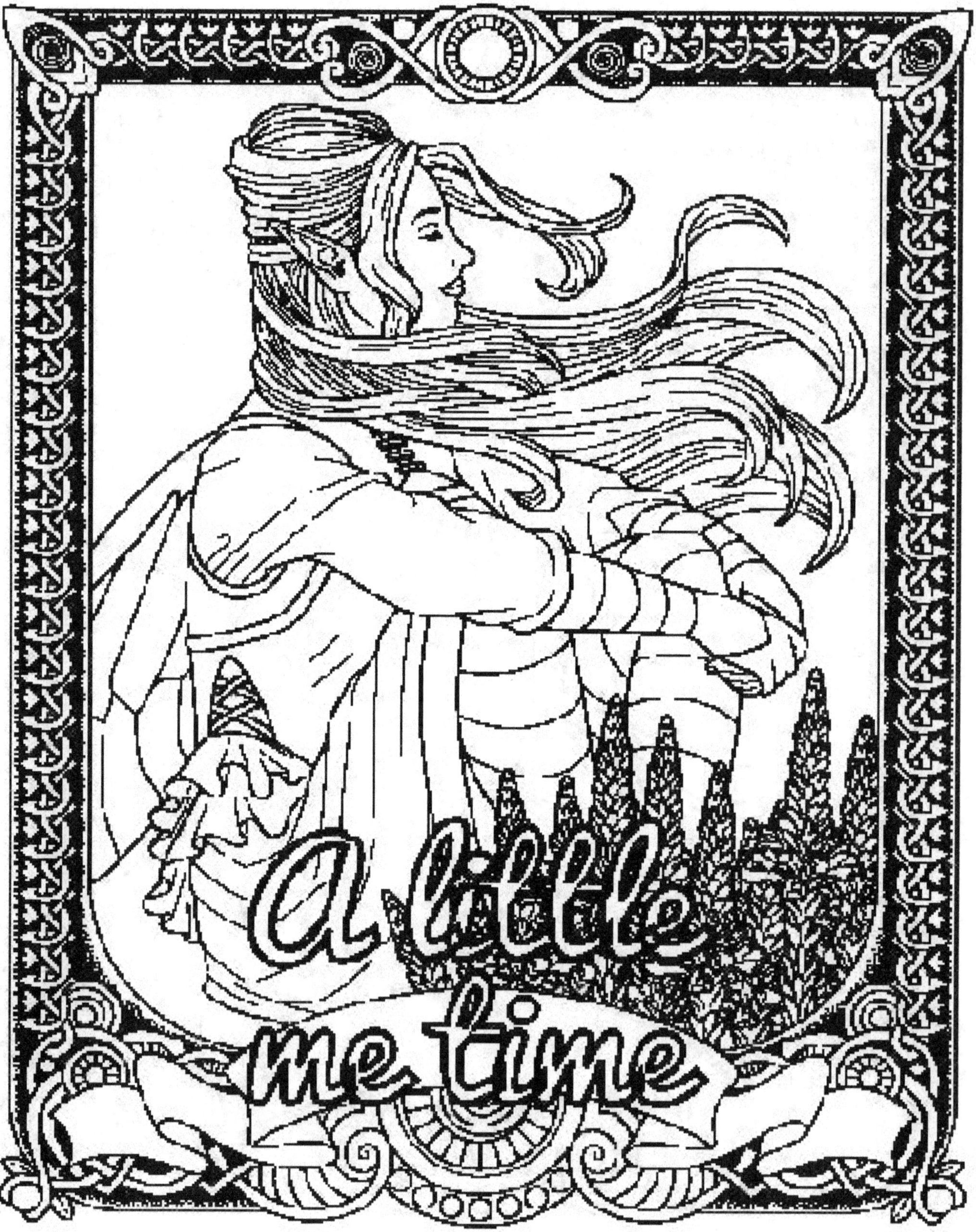
A little
me time

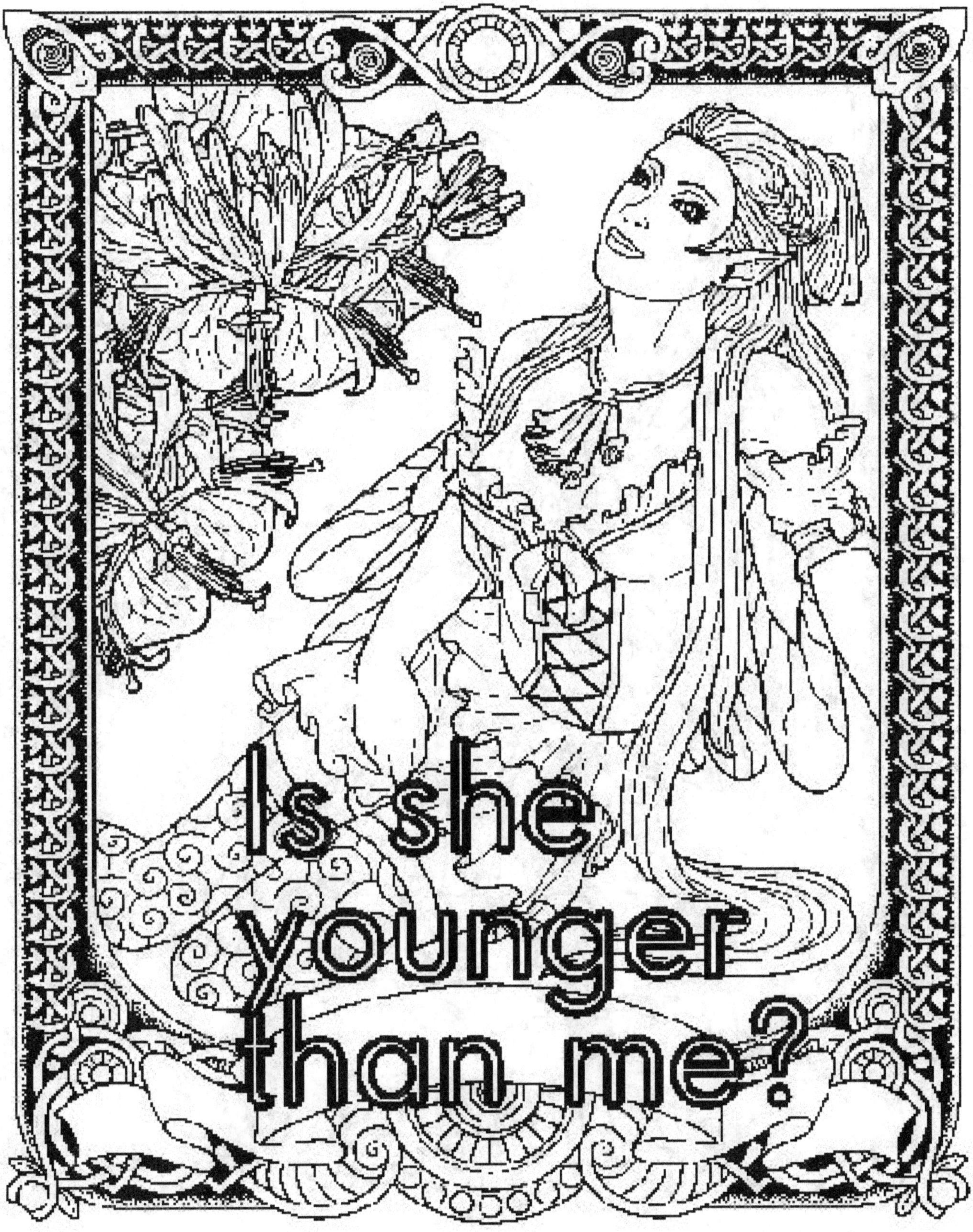
Is she younger than me?

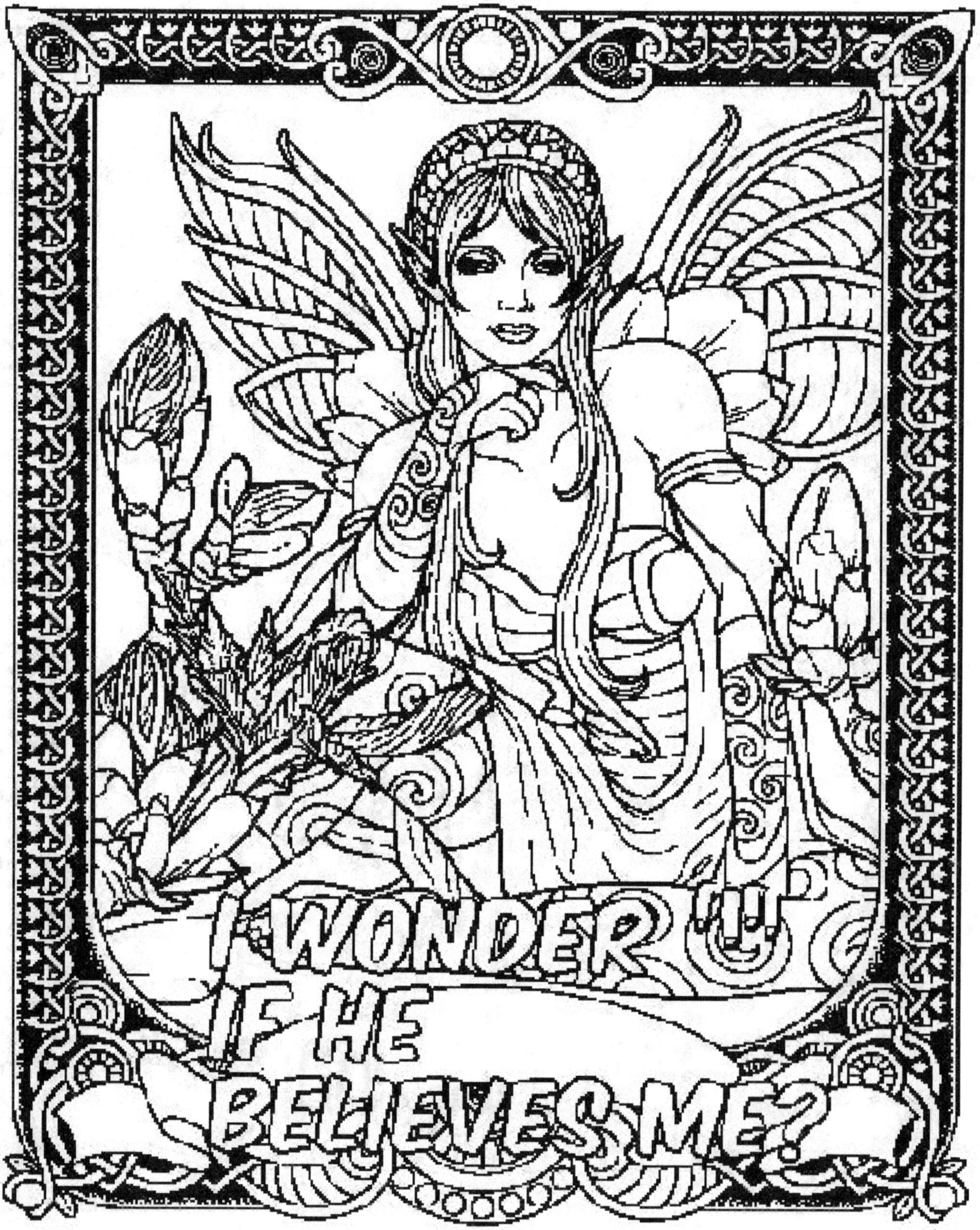
I WONDER "!"
IF HE
BELIEVES ME?

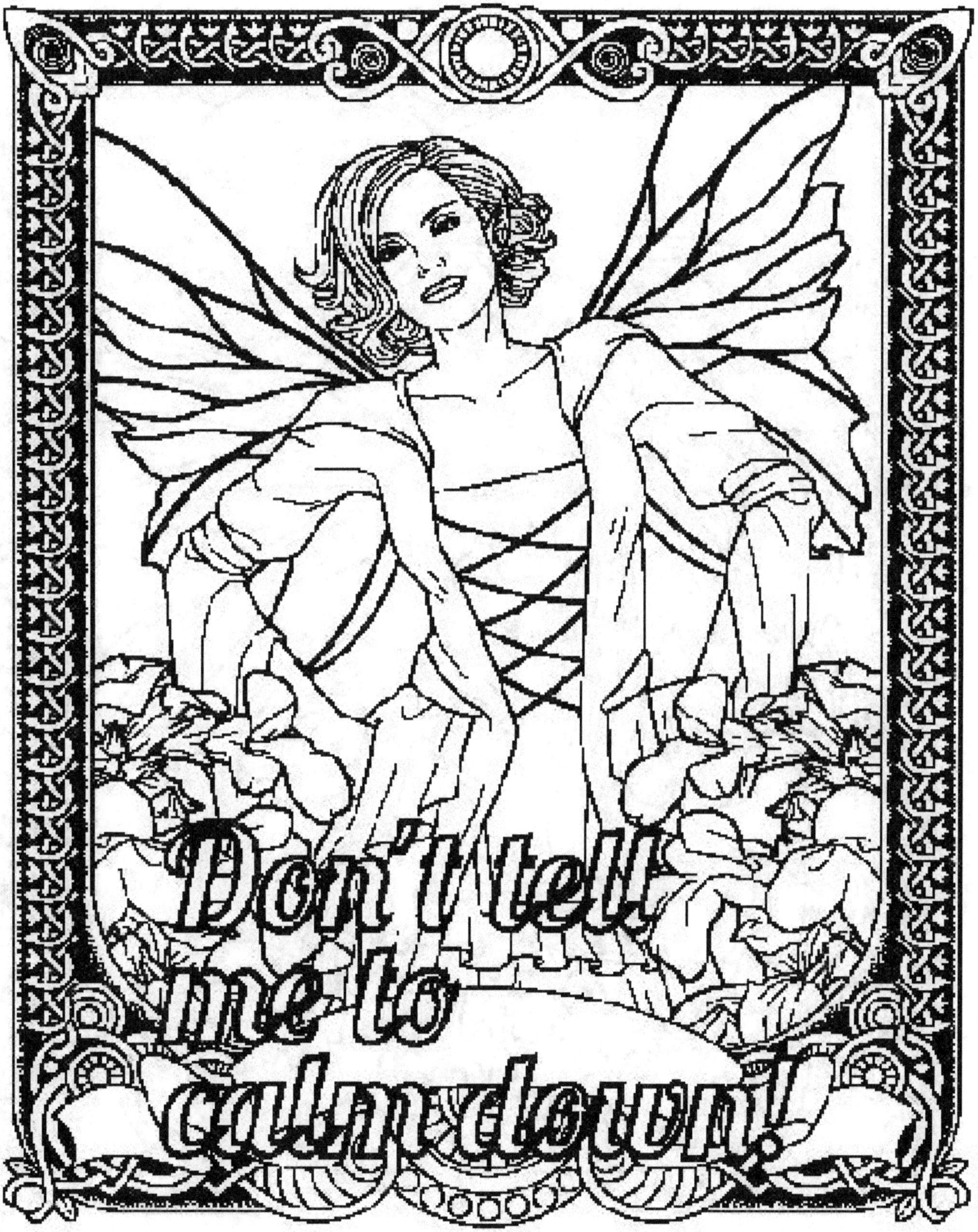
Don't tell
me to
calm down!

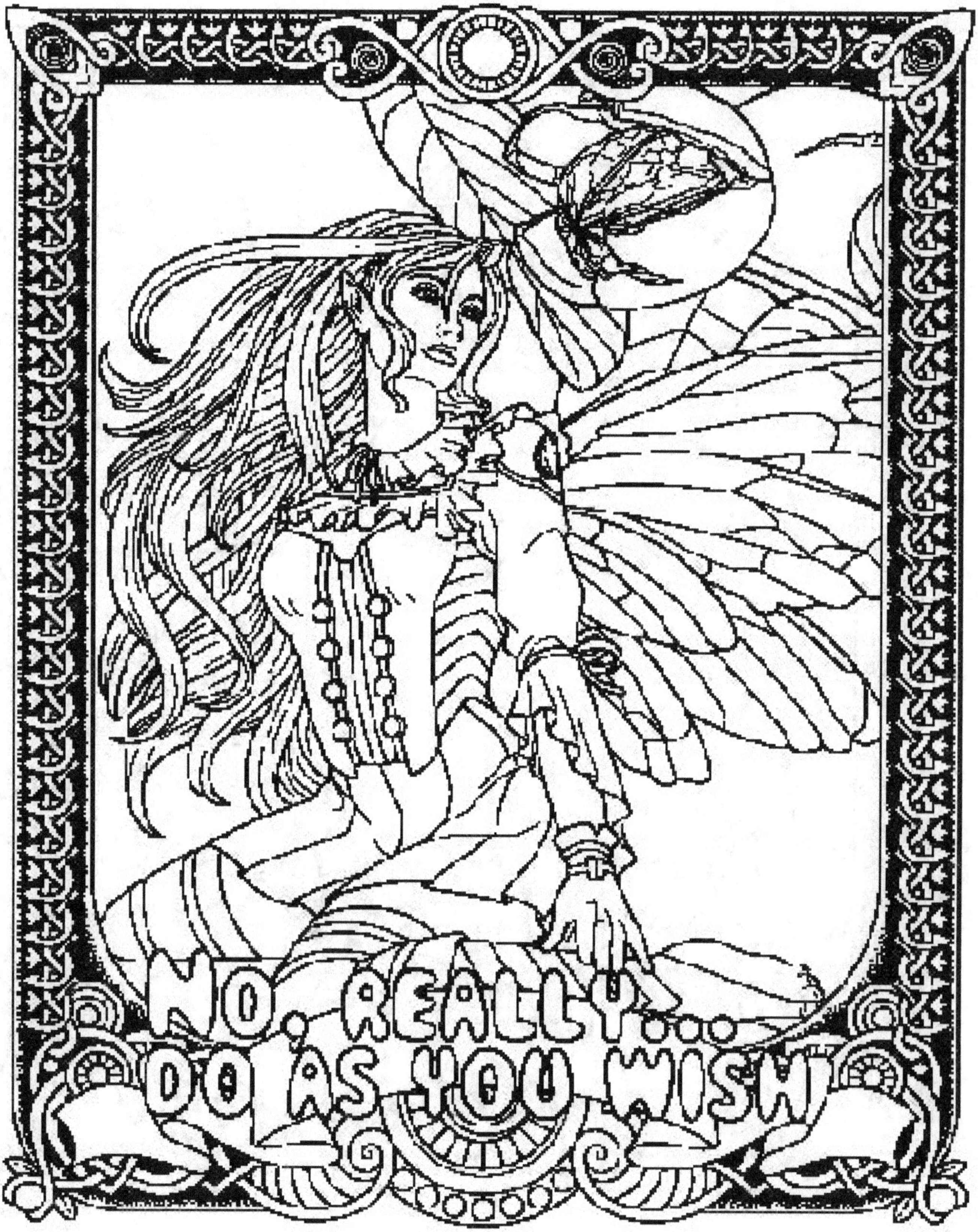
NO, REALLY....
DO AS YOU WISH

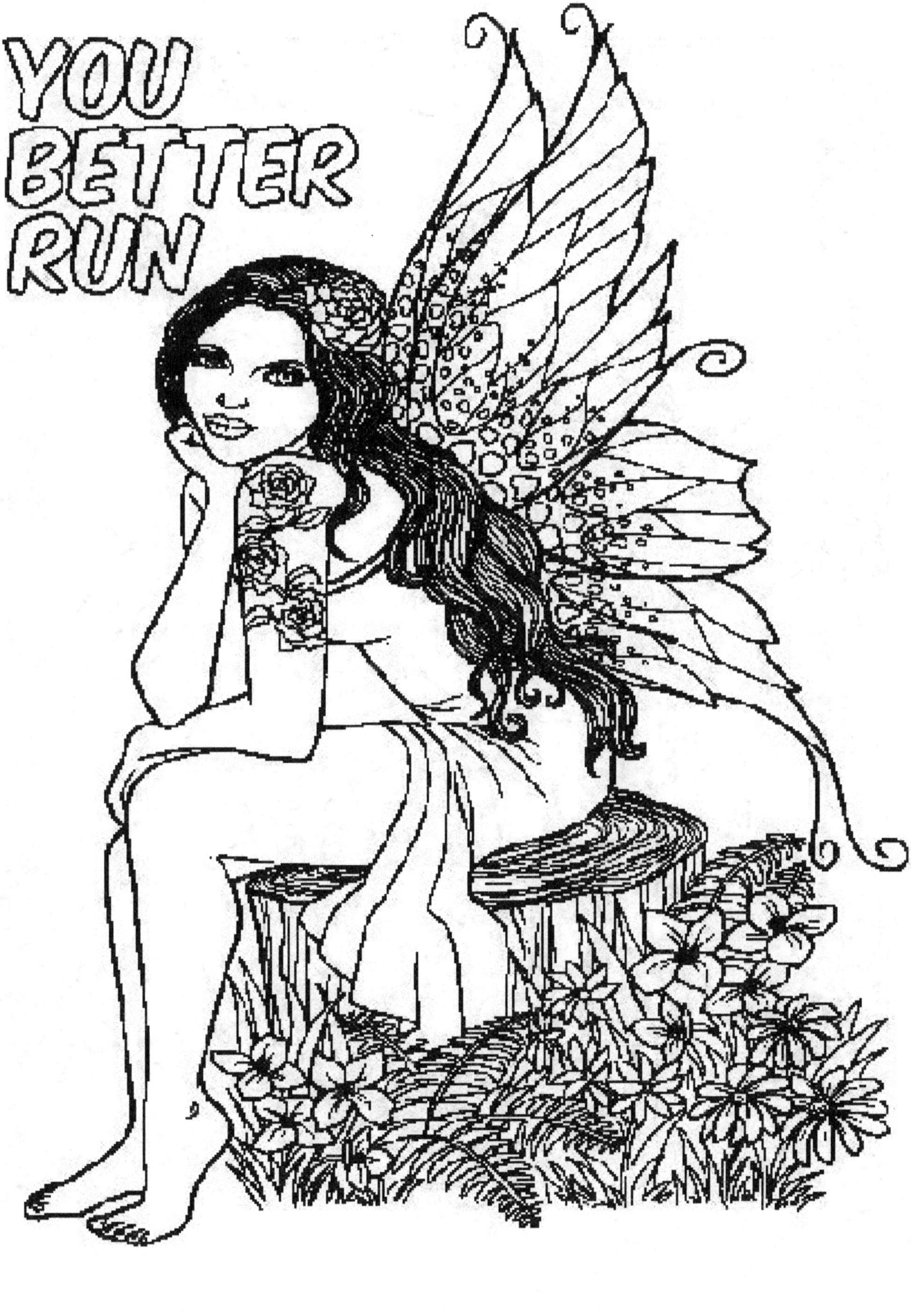
YOU
BETTER
RUN

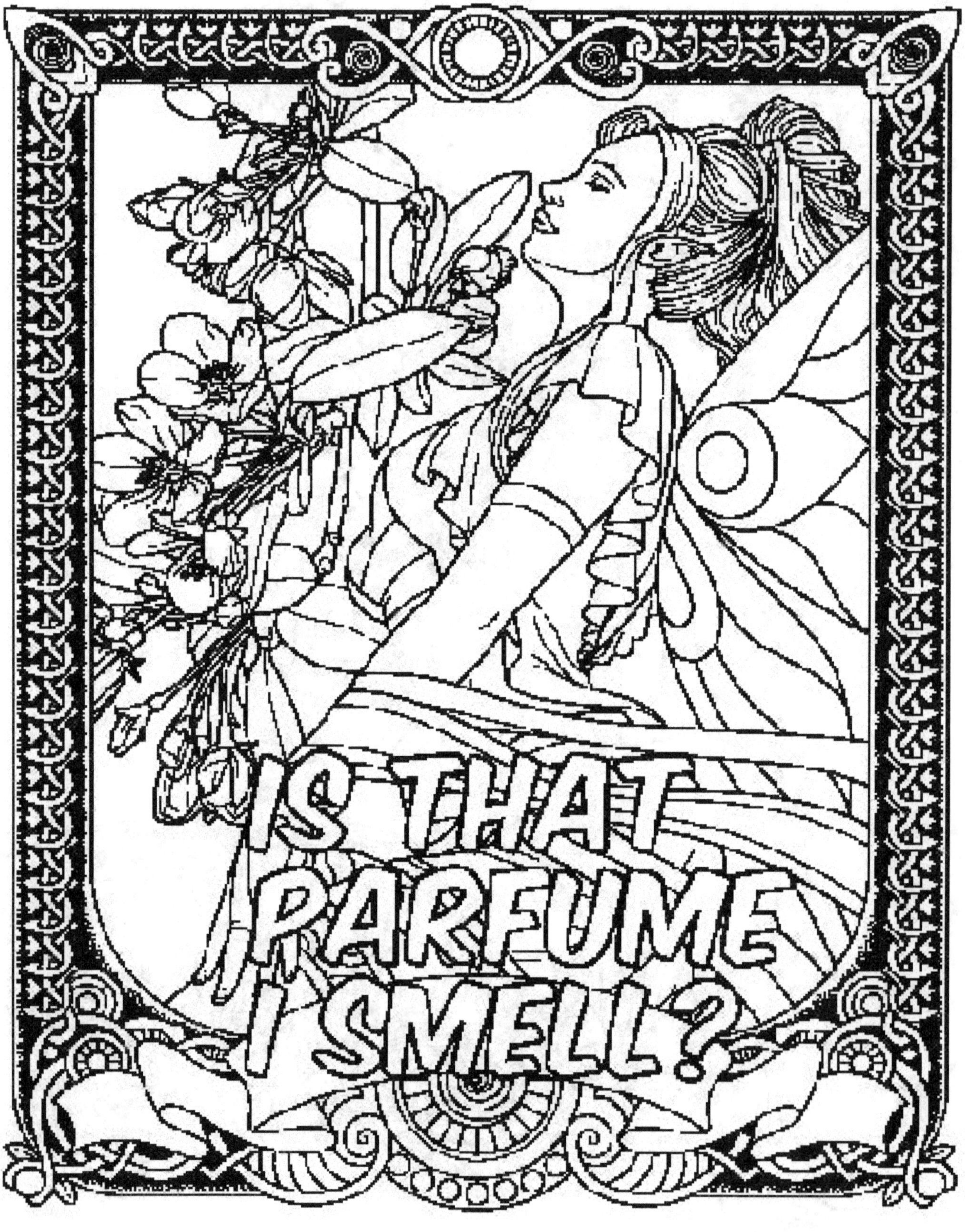
IS THAT
PARFUME
I SMELL?

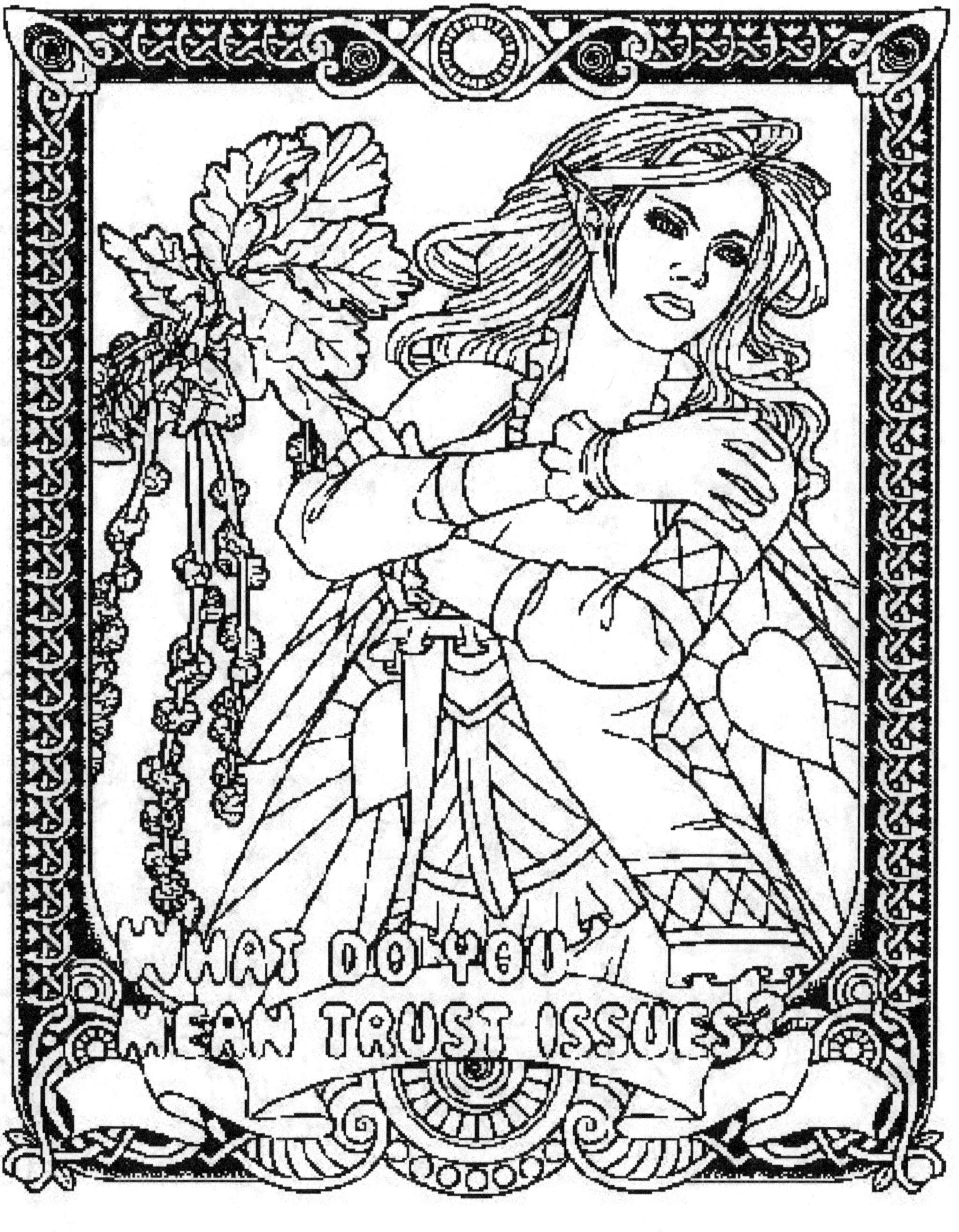
WHAT DO YOU
MEAN TRUST ISSUES?

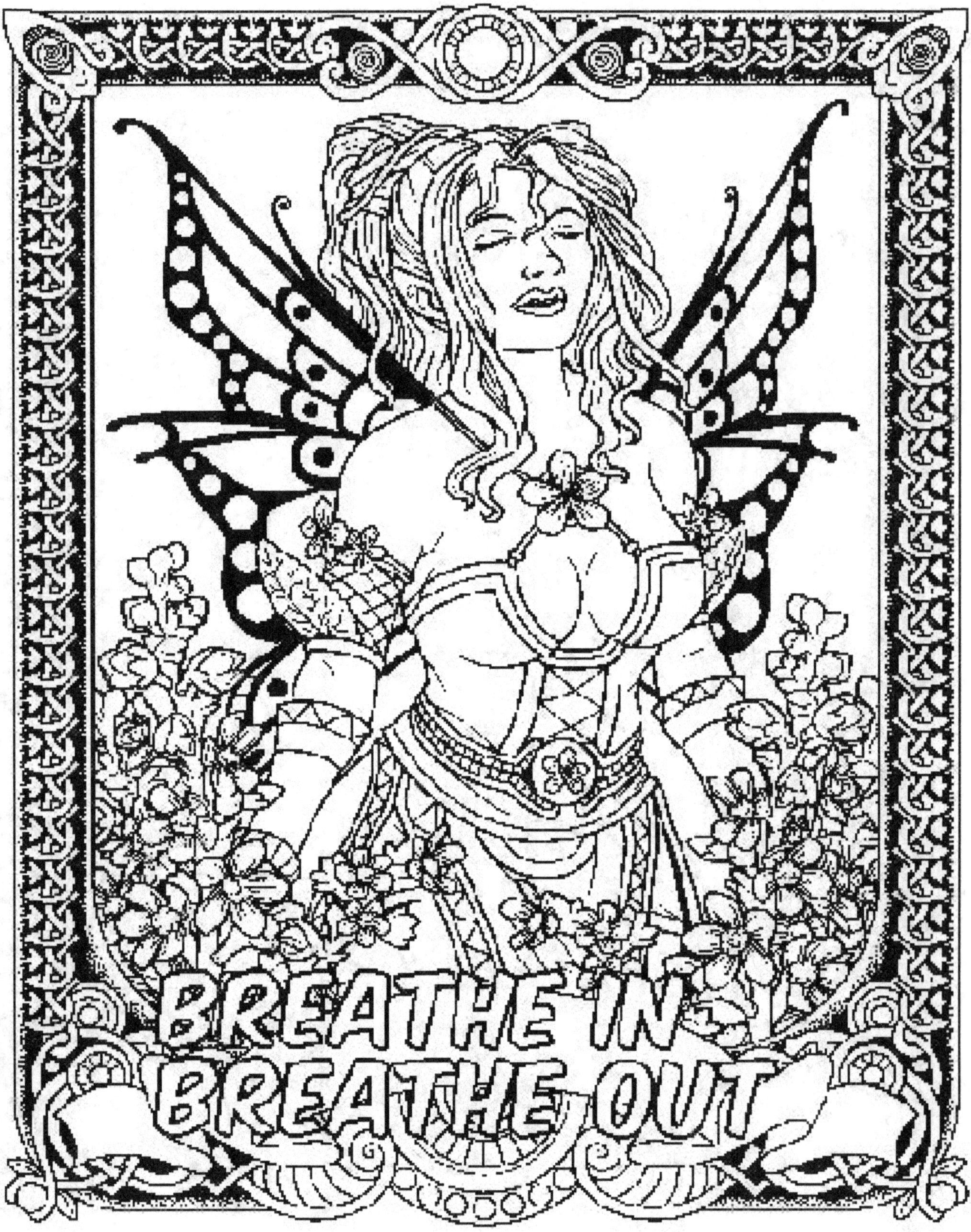
BREATHE IN
BREATHE OUT

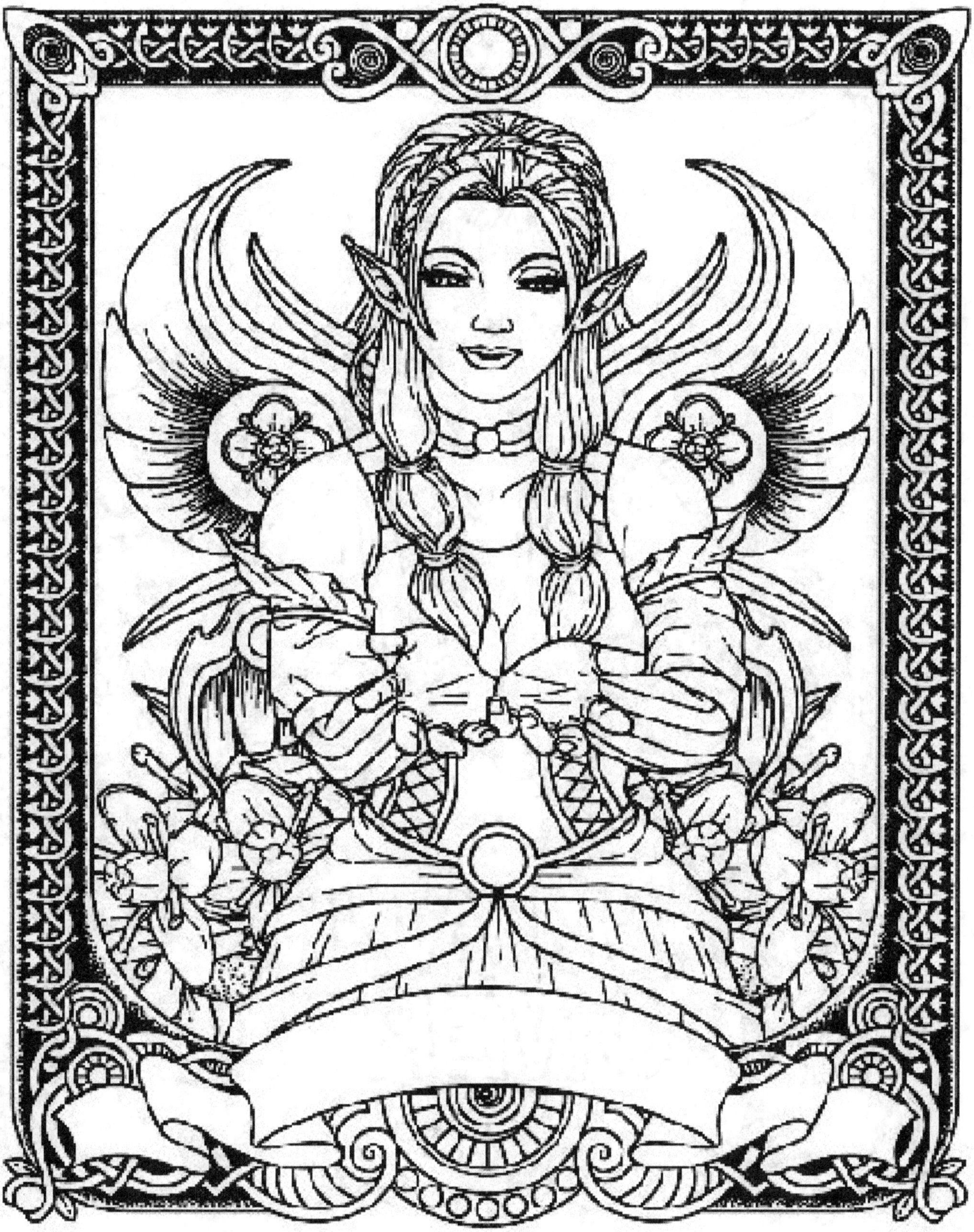

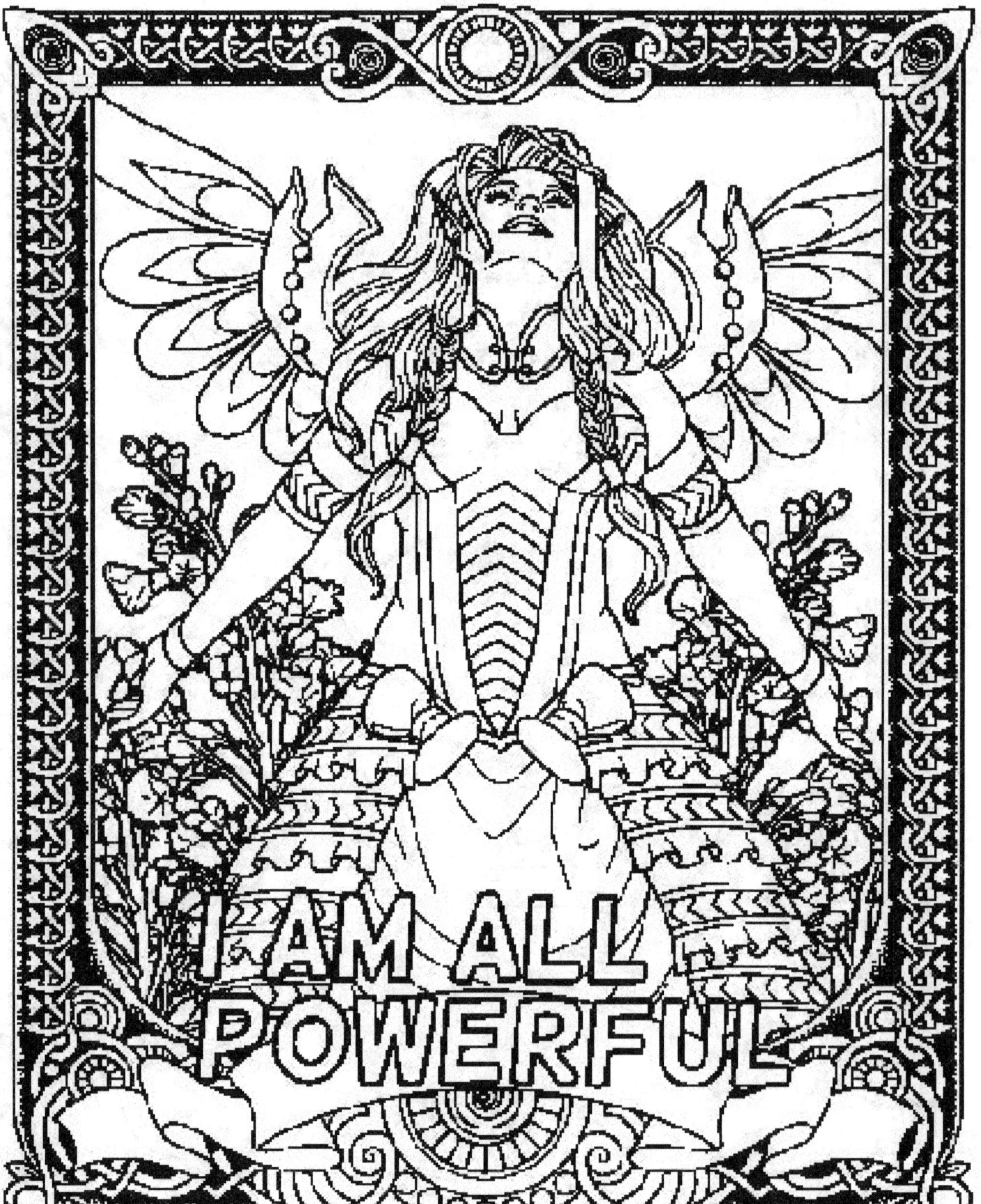
I AM ALL
POWERFUL

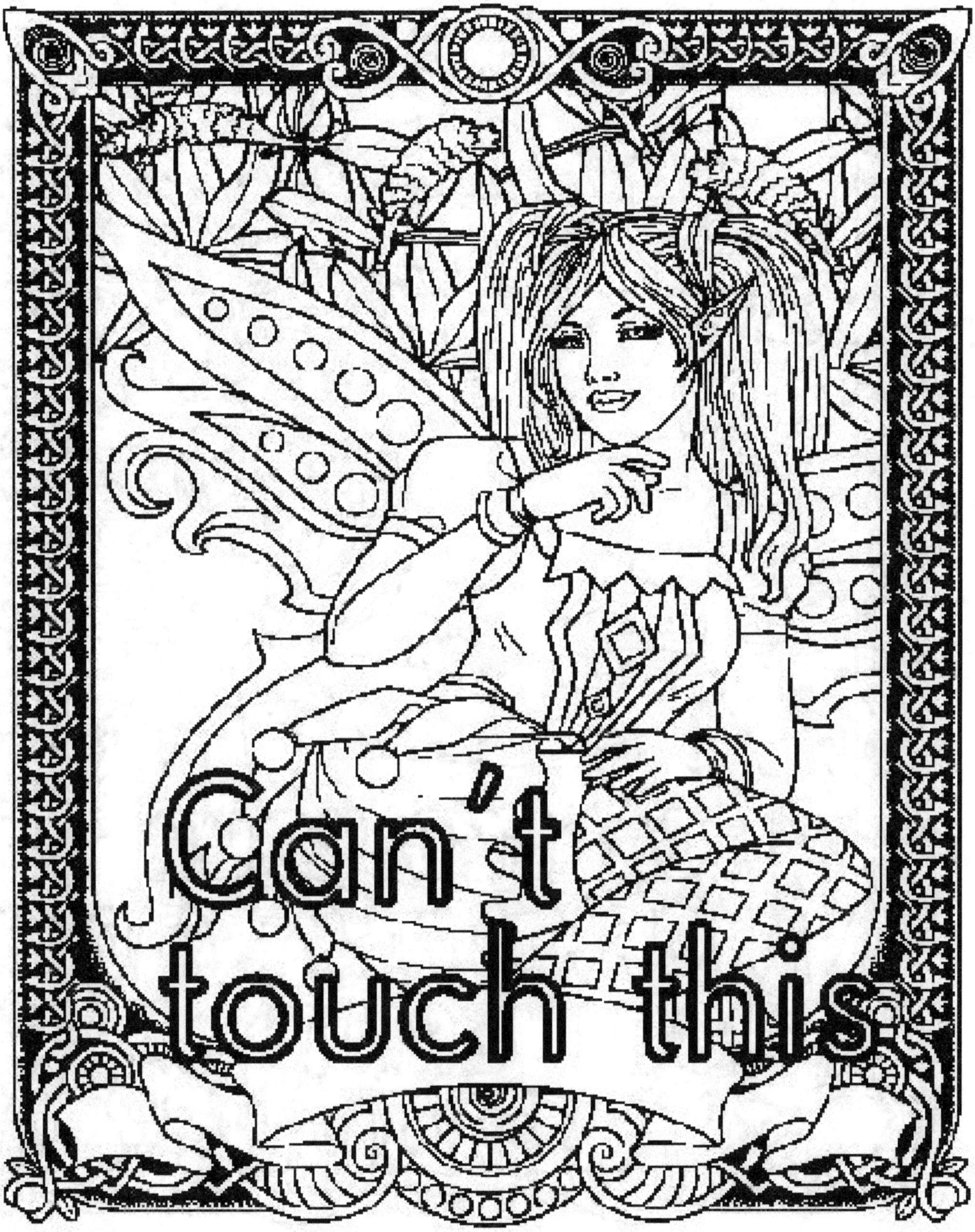
Can't
touch this

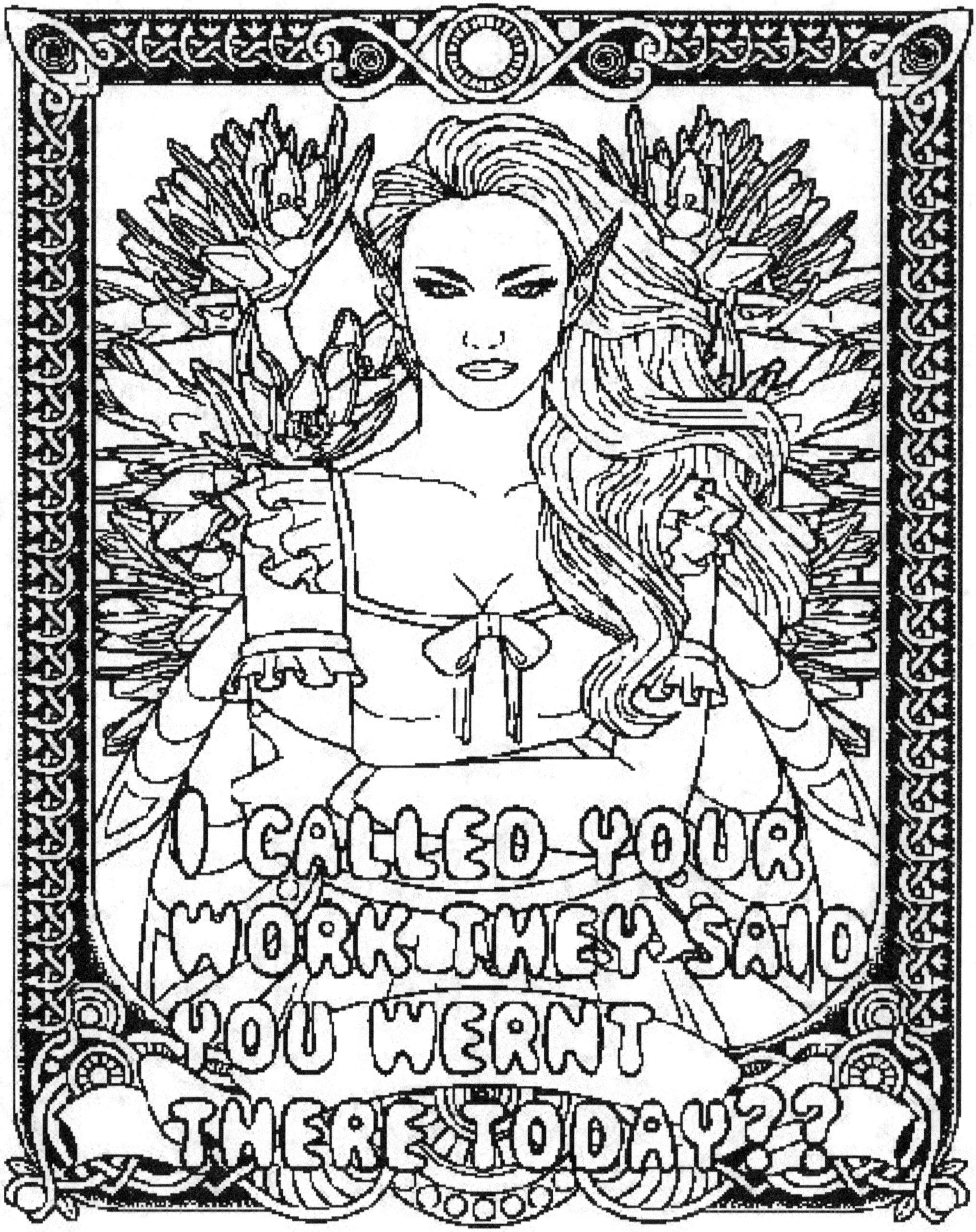
I CALLED YOUR
WORK THEY SAID
YOU WERNT
THERE TODAY??

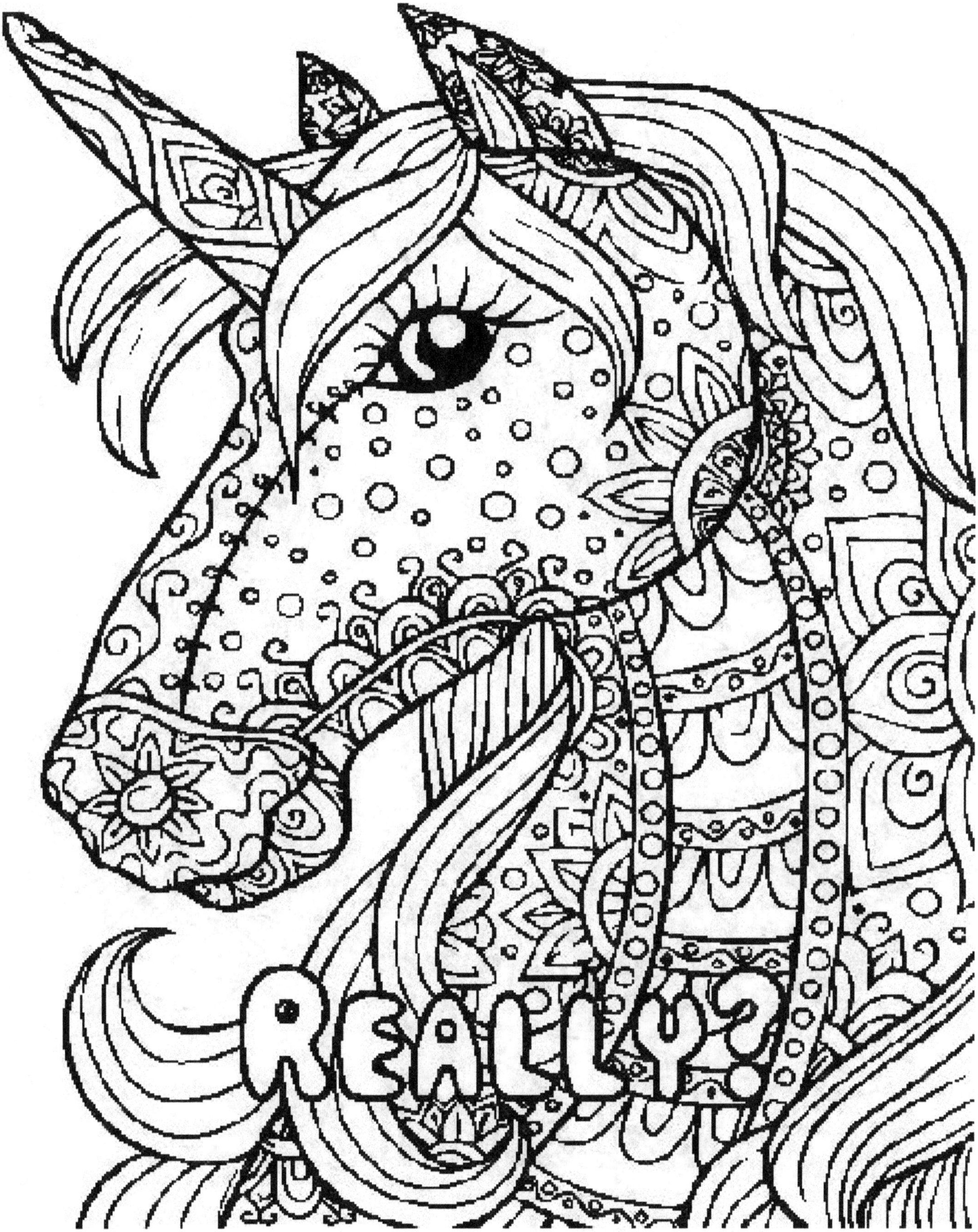
REALLY?

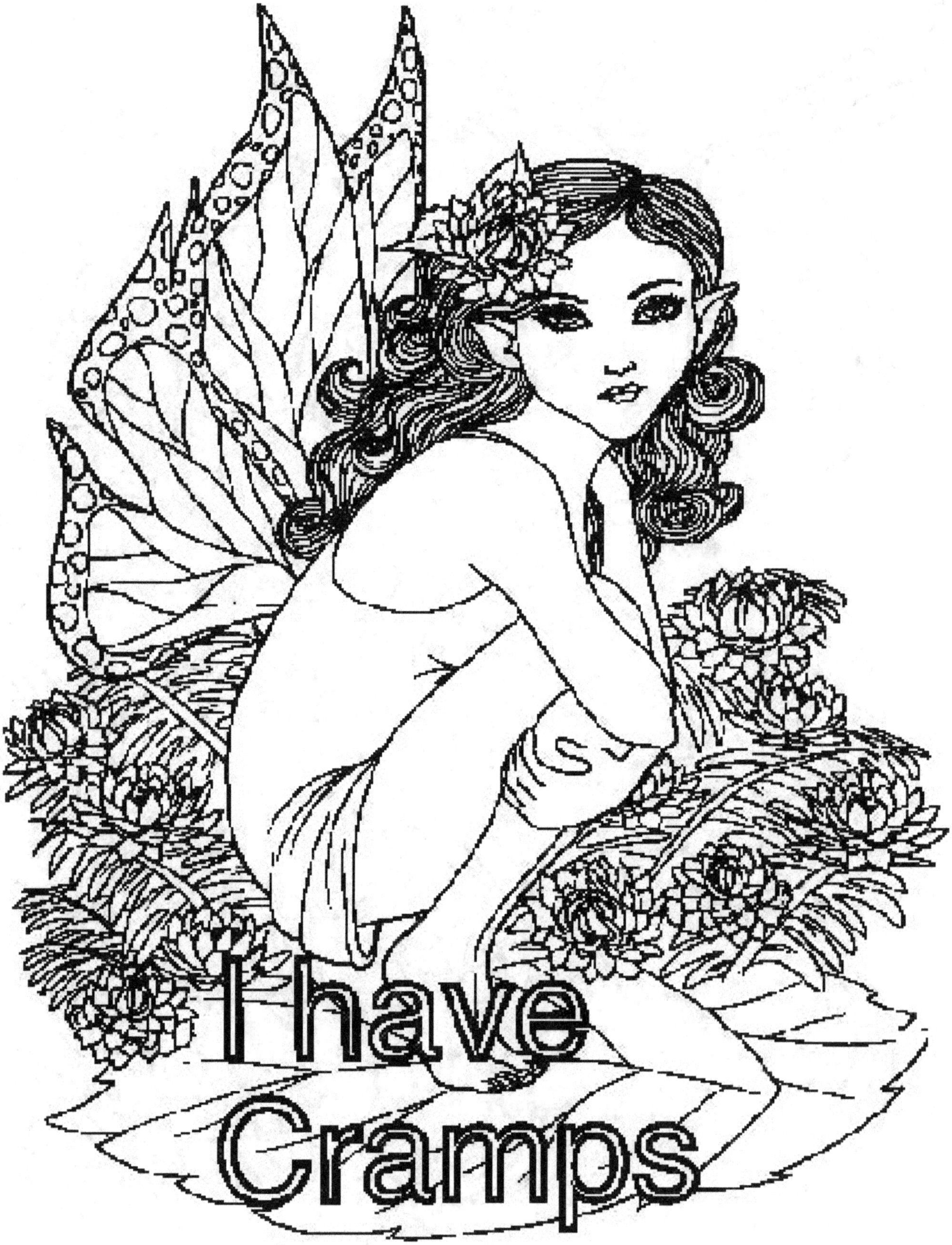
I have
Cramps

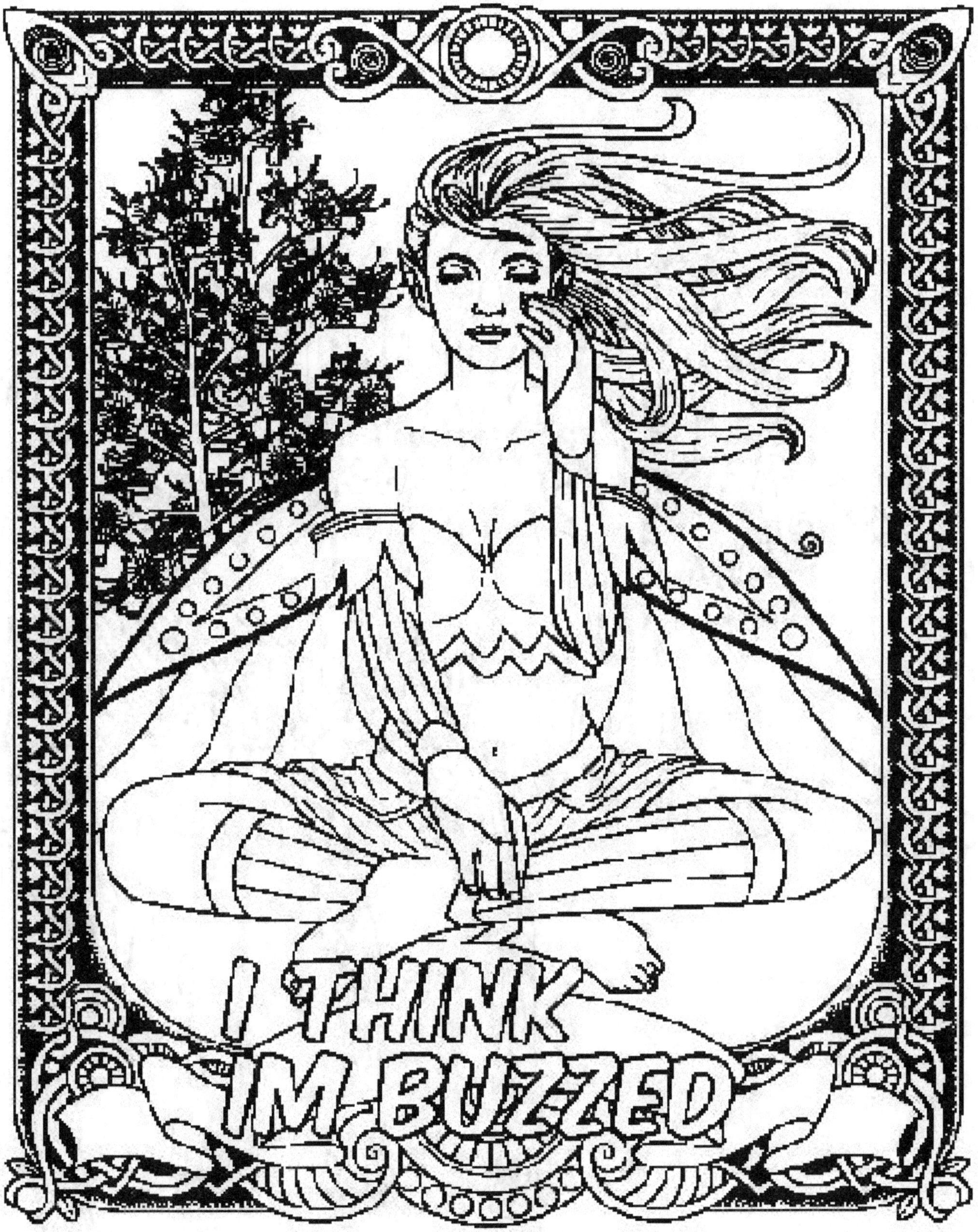
I THINK
IM BUZZED

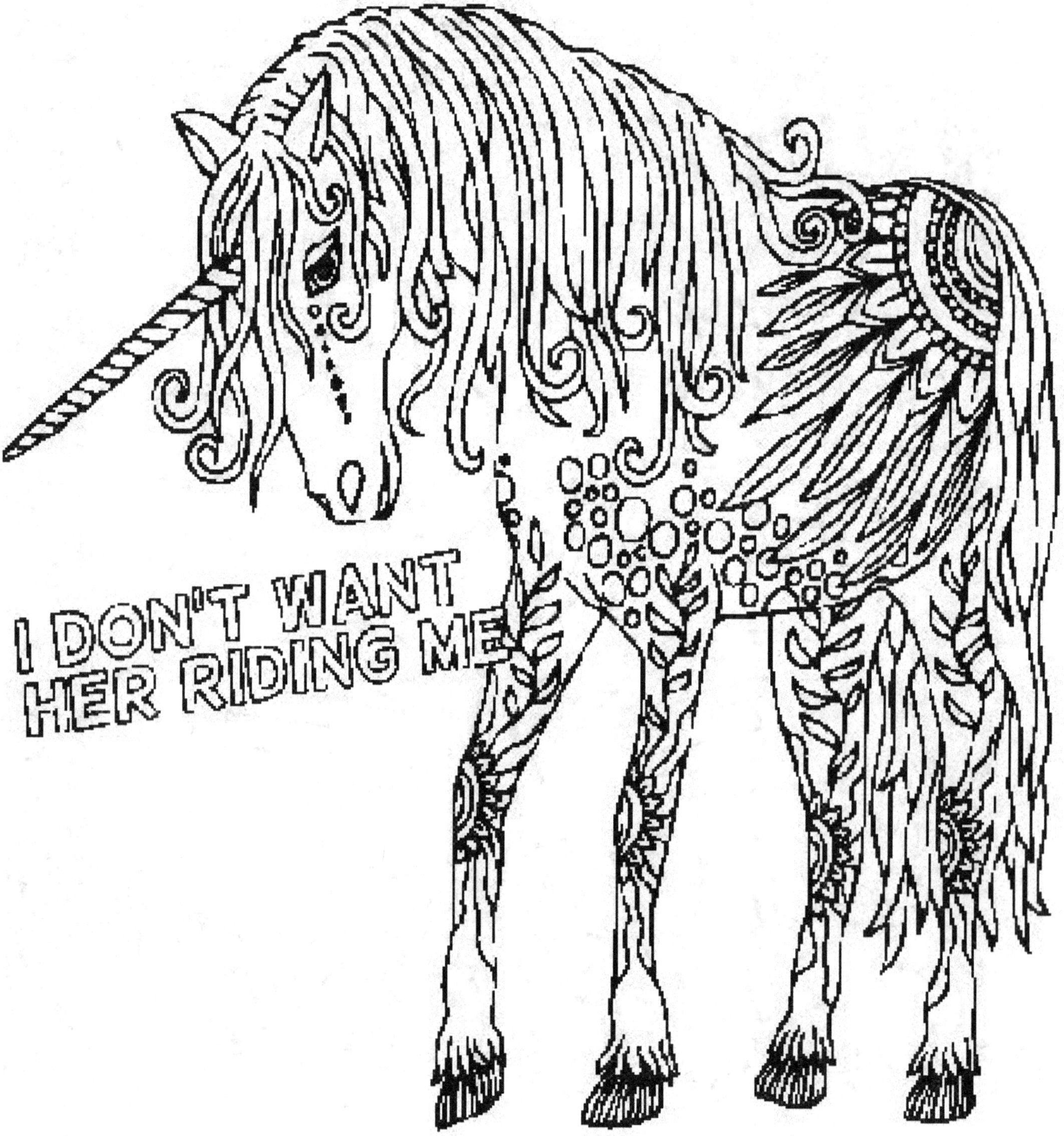
I DON'T WANT
HER RIDING ME

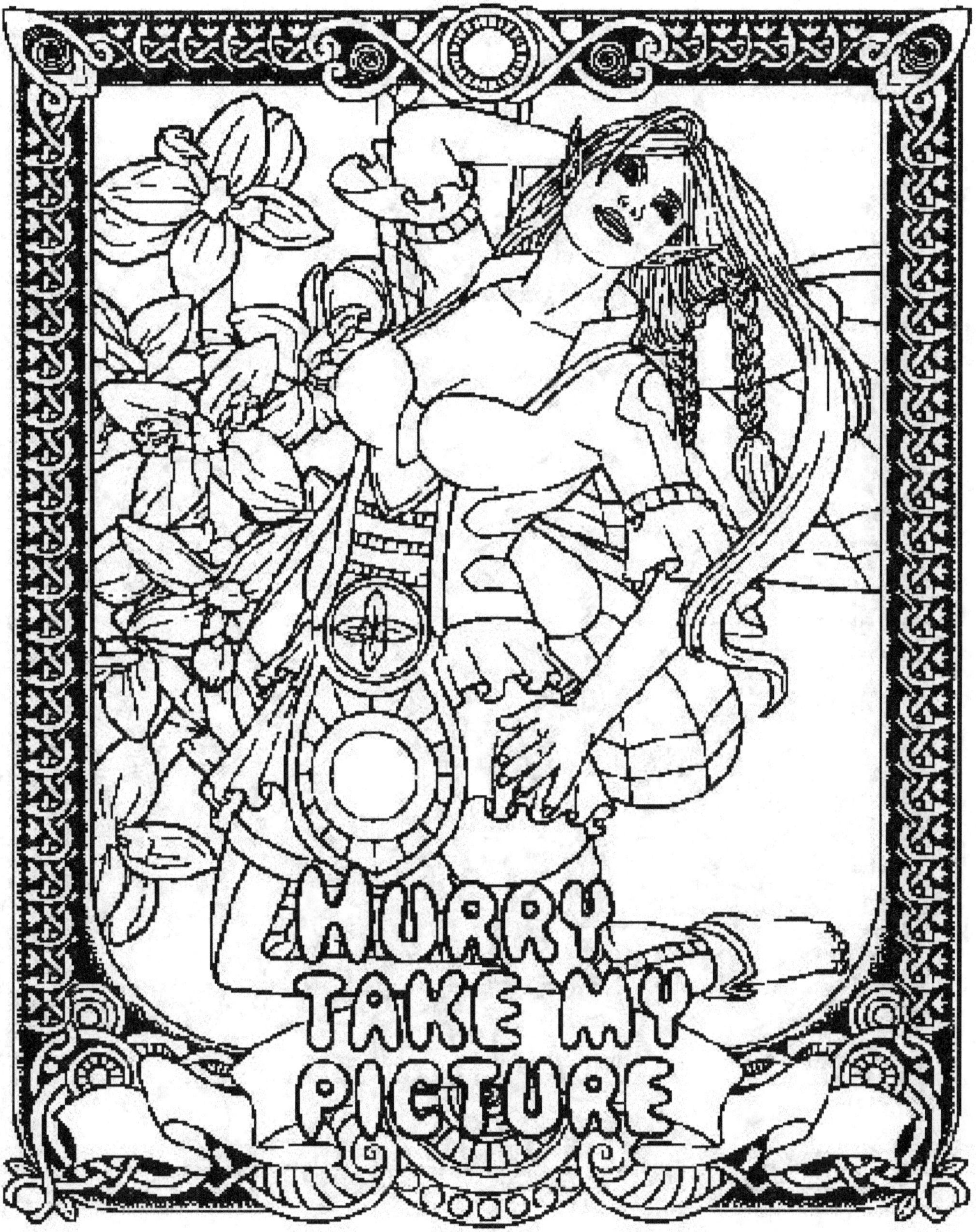
HURRY
TAKE MY
PICTURE

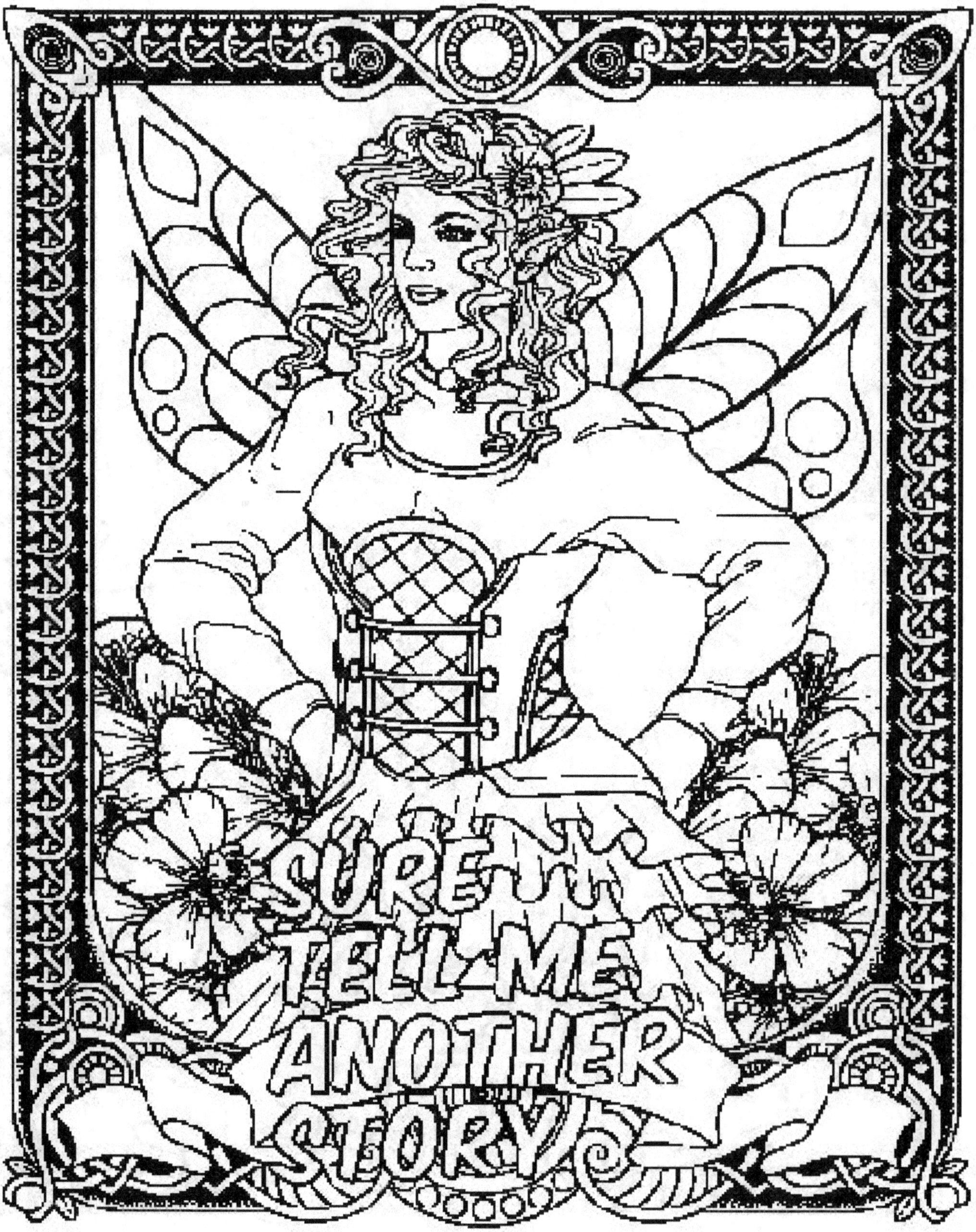
SURE
TELL ME
ANOTHER
STORY

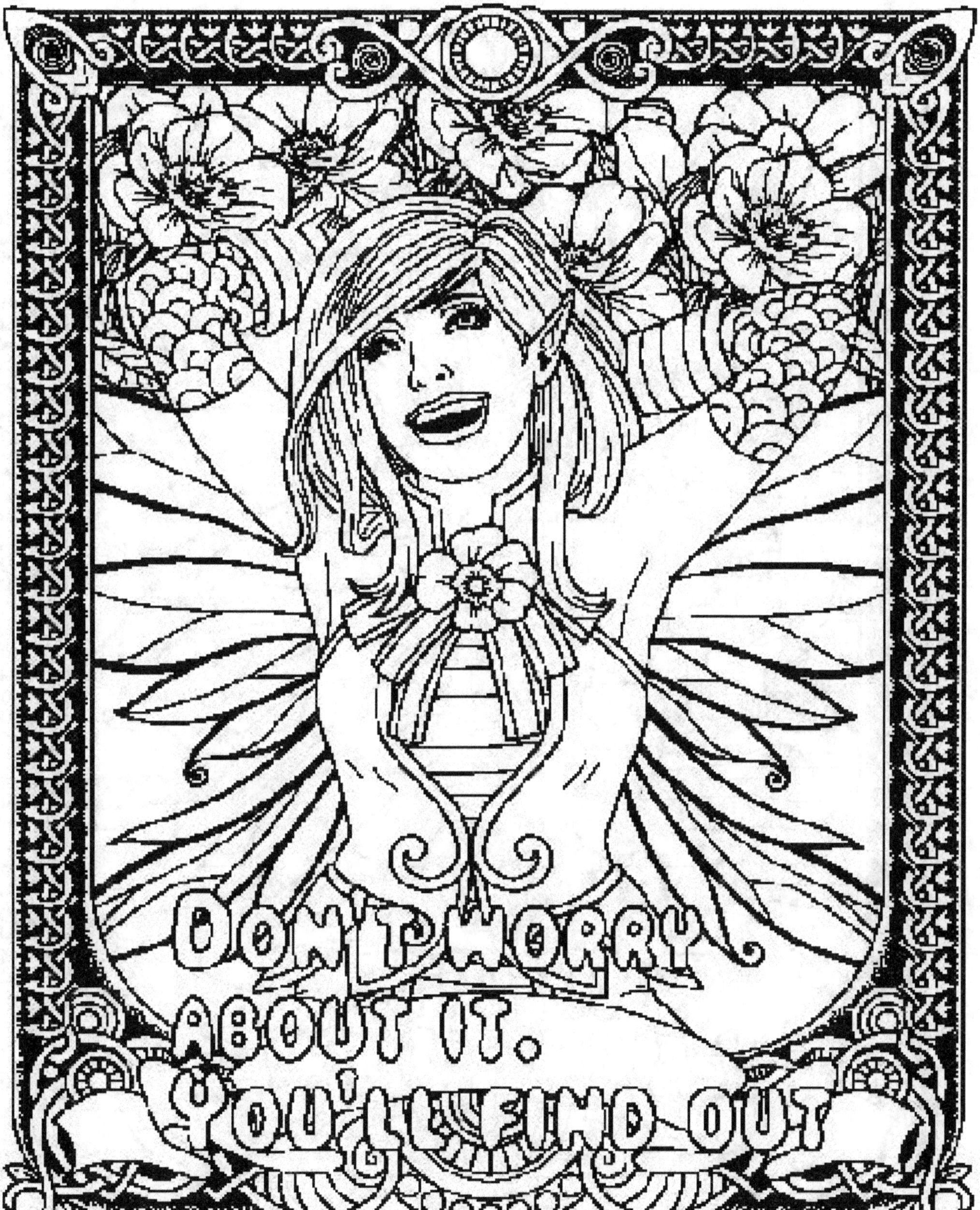
DON'T WORRY
ABOUT IT.
YOU'LL FIND OUT

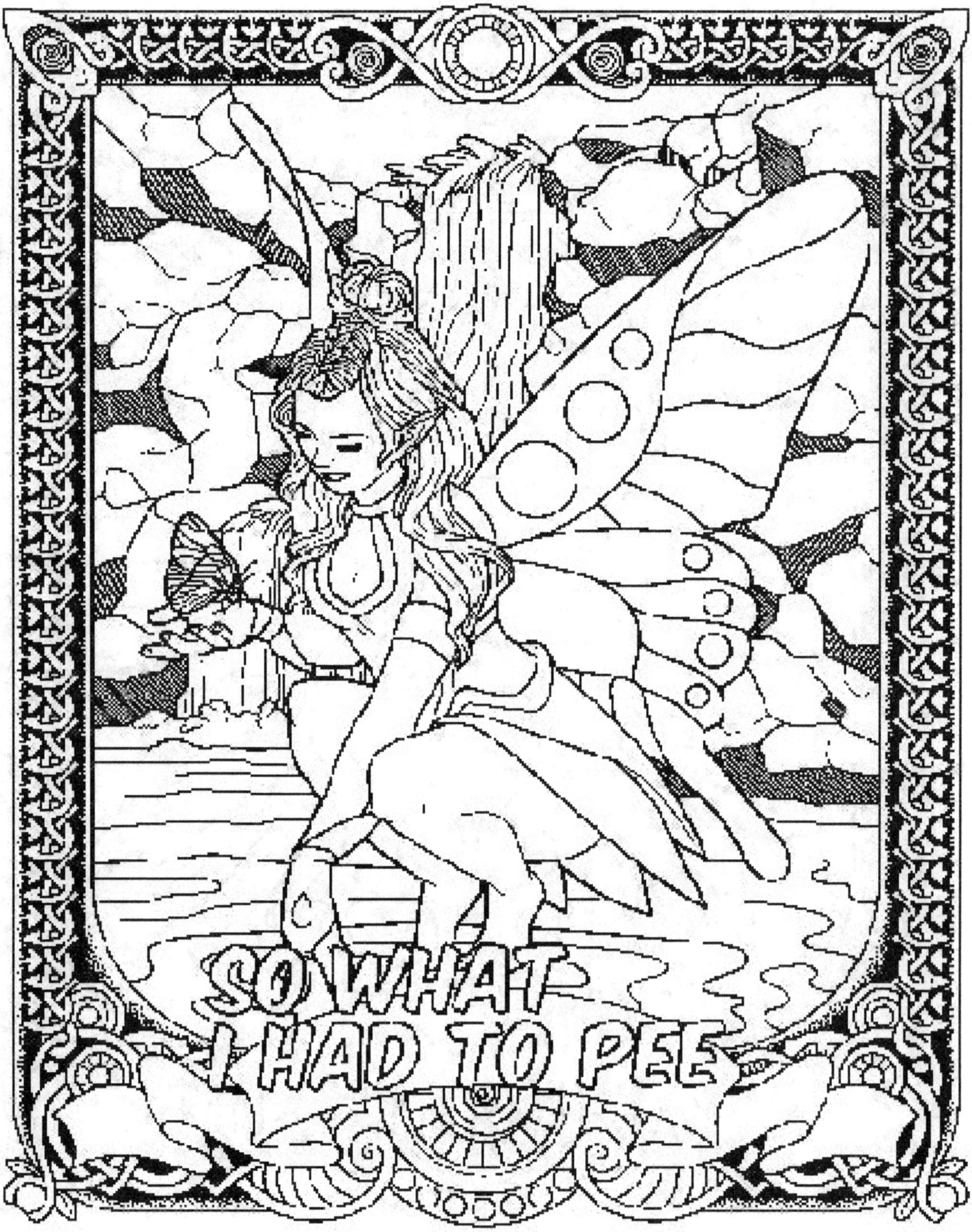
SO WHAT
I HAD TO PEE

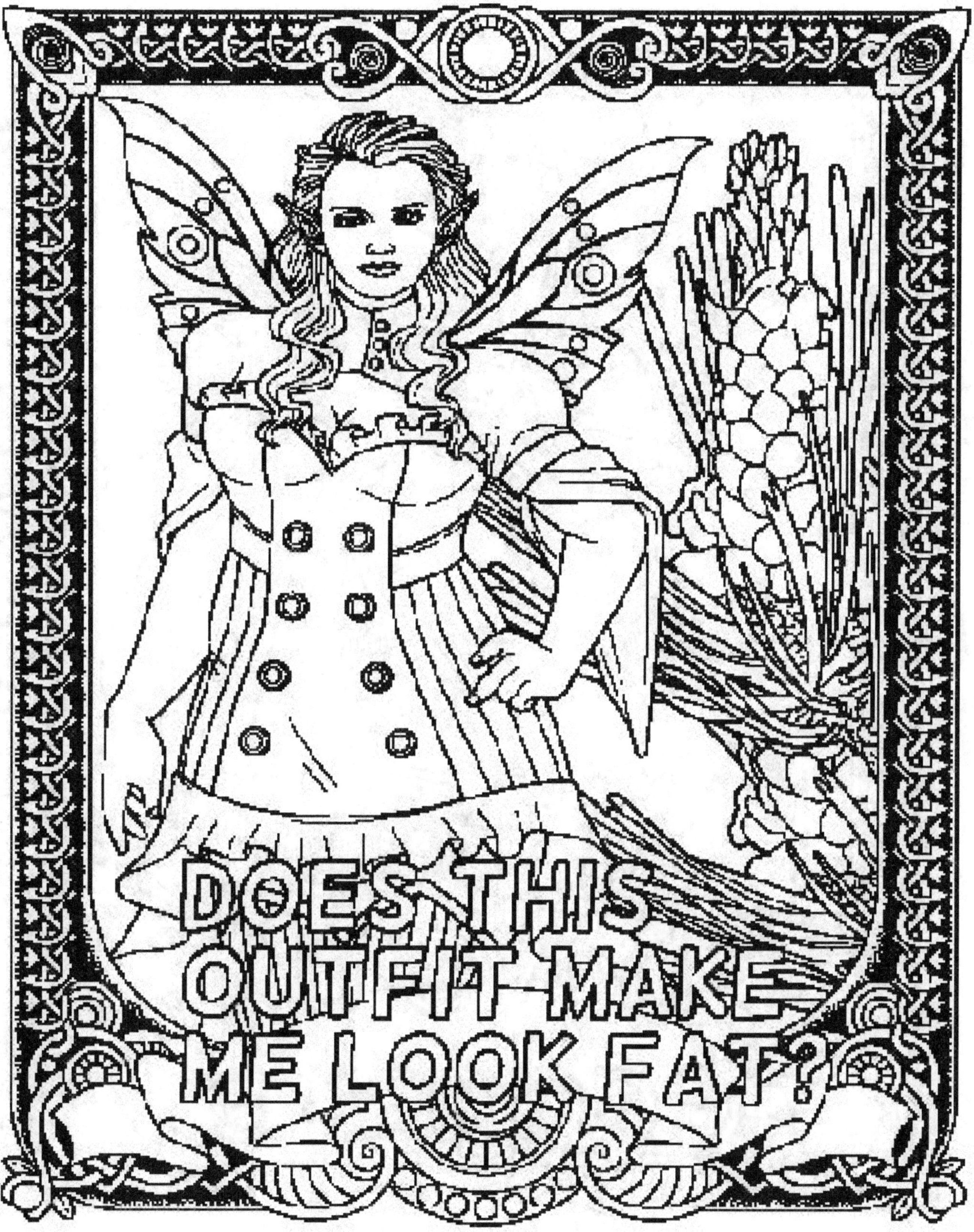
DOES THIS
OUTFIT MAKE
ME LOOK FAT?

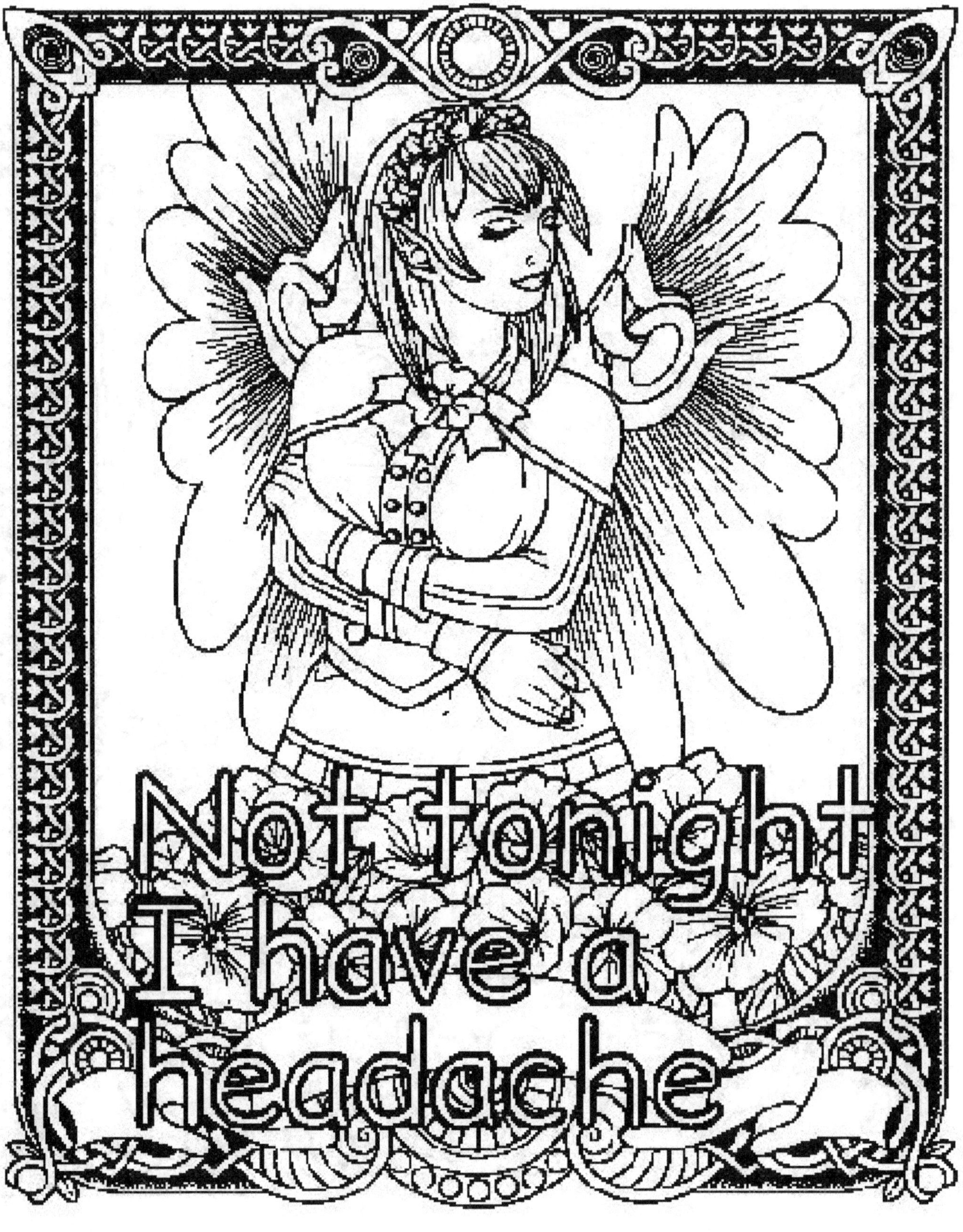
Not tonight
I have a
headache

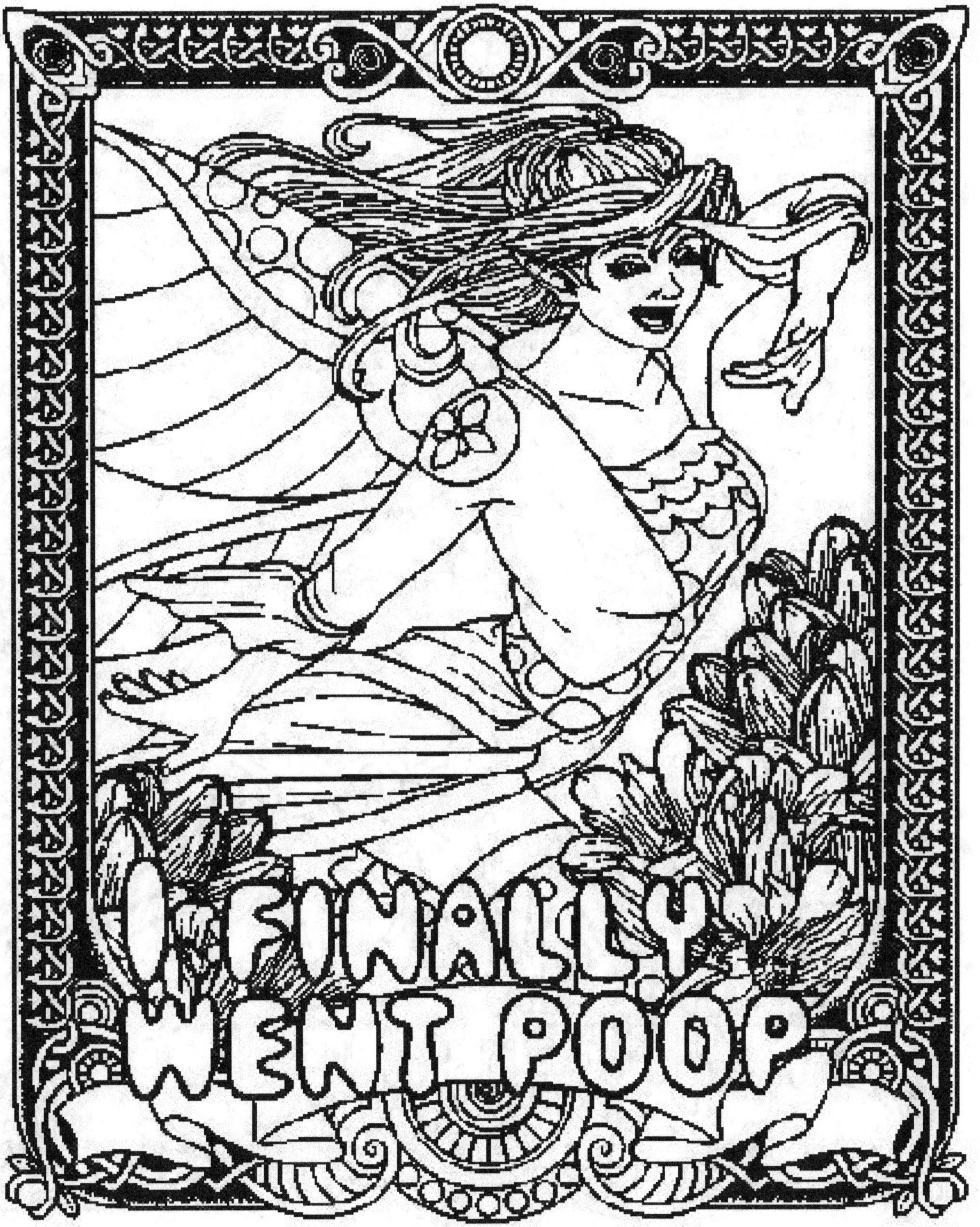
I FINALLY WENT POOP

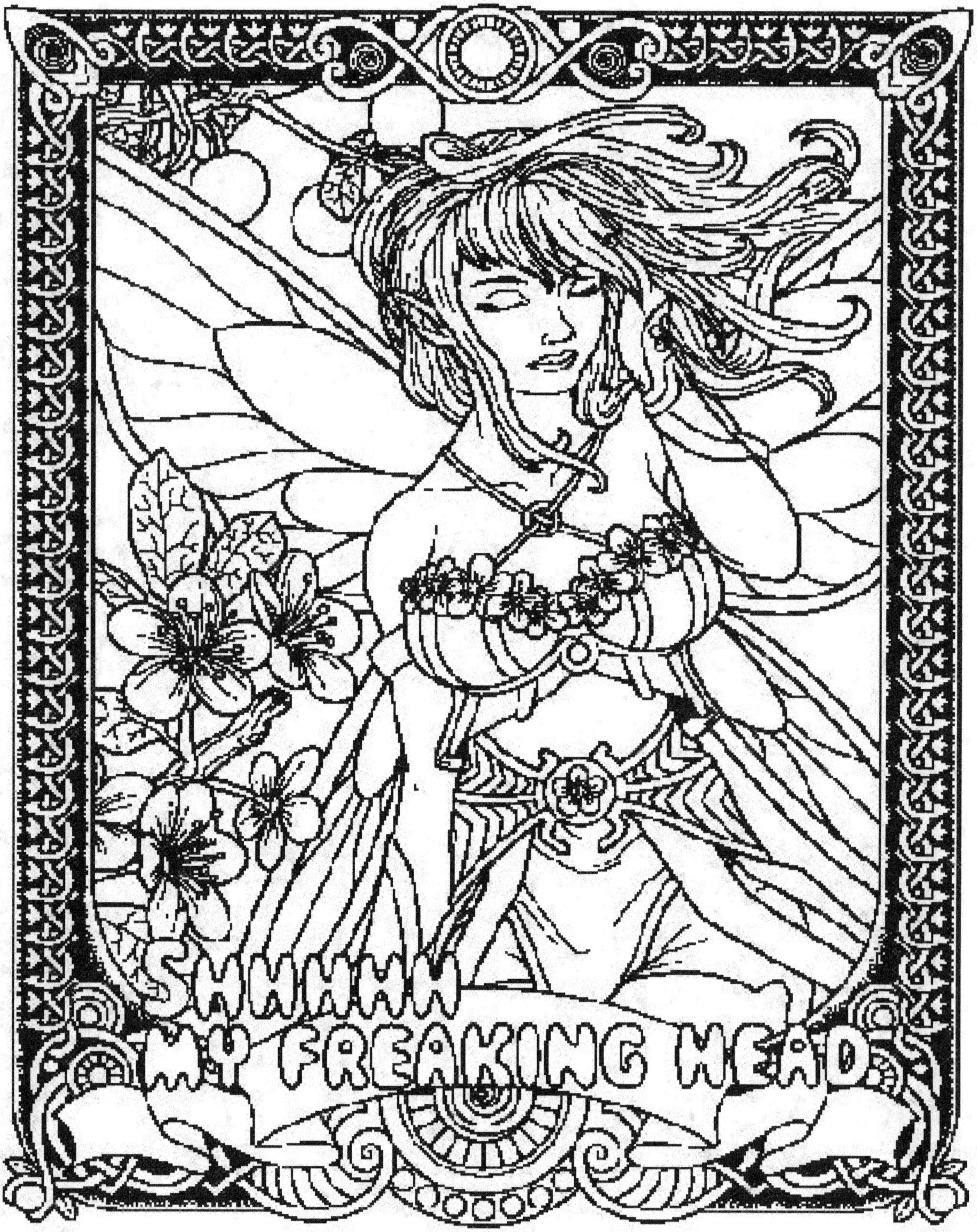
SHHHHH
MY FREAKING HEAD

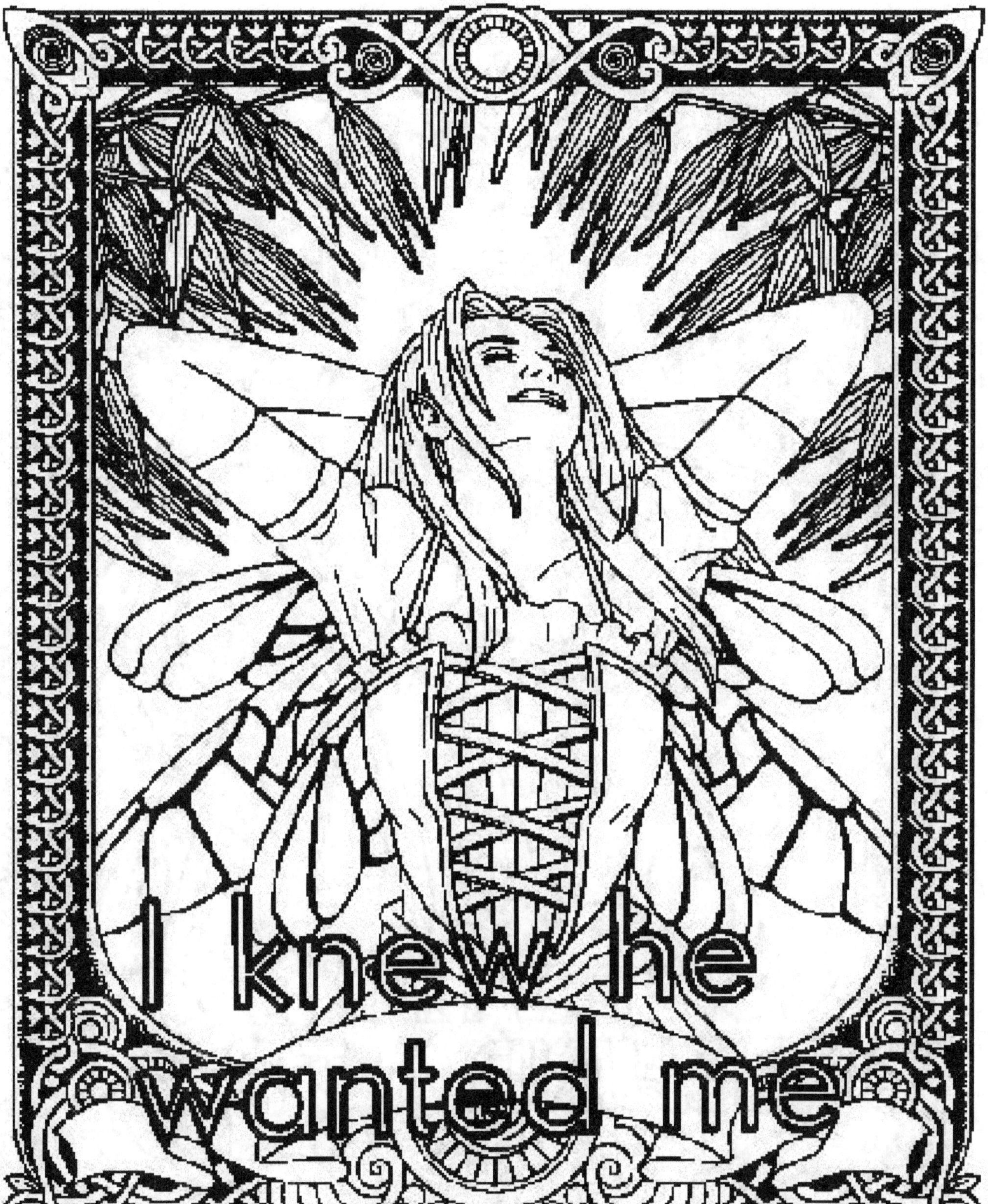
I knew he
wanted me

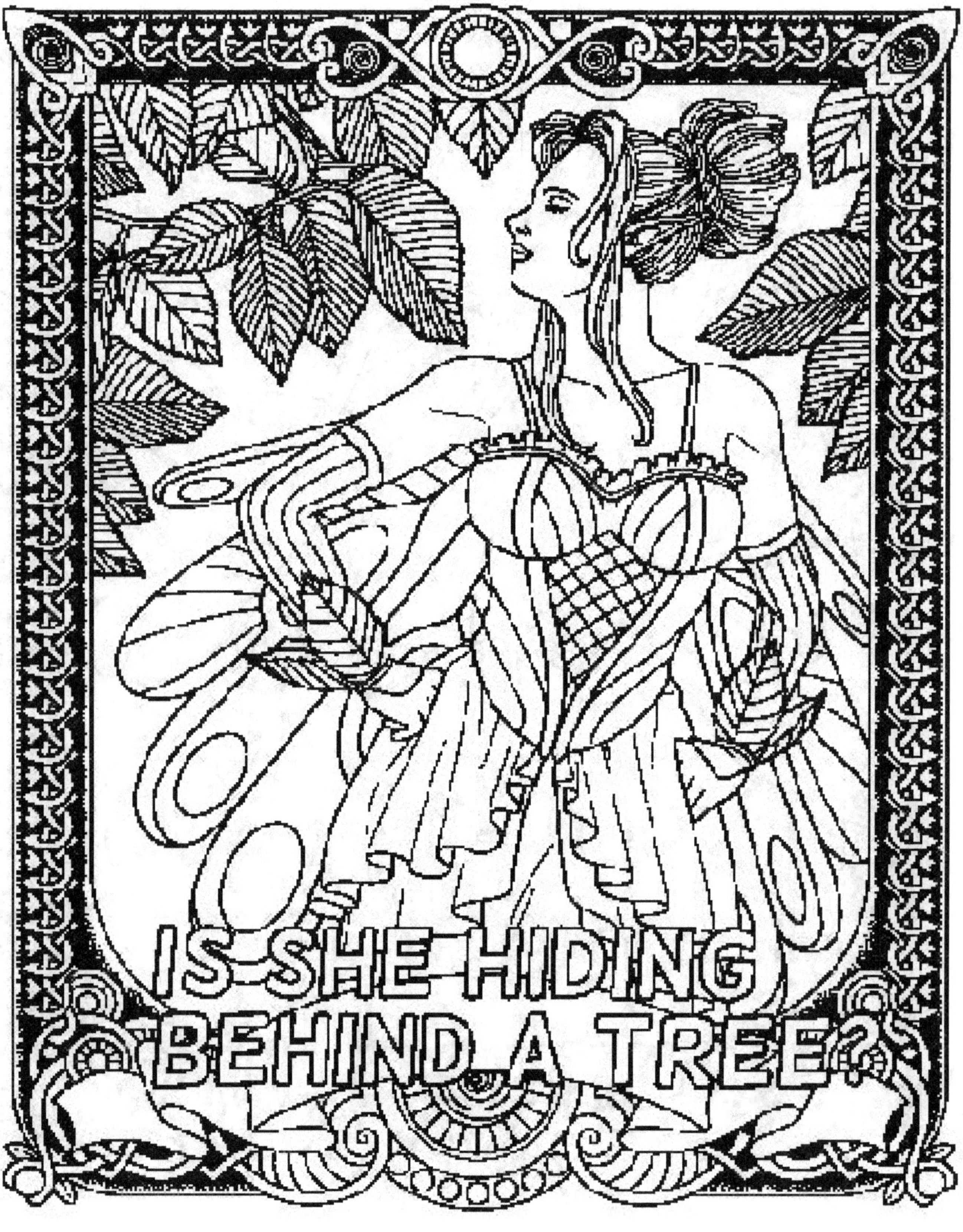
IS SHE HIDING
BEHIND A TREE?

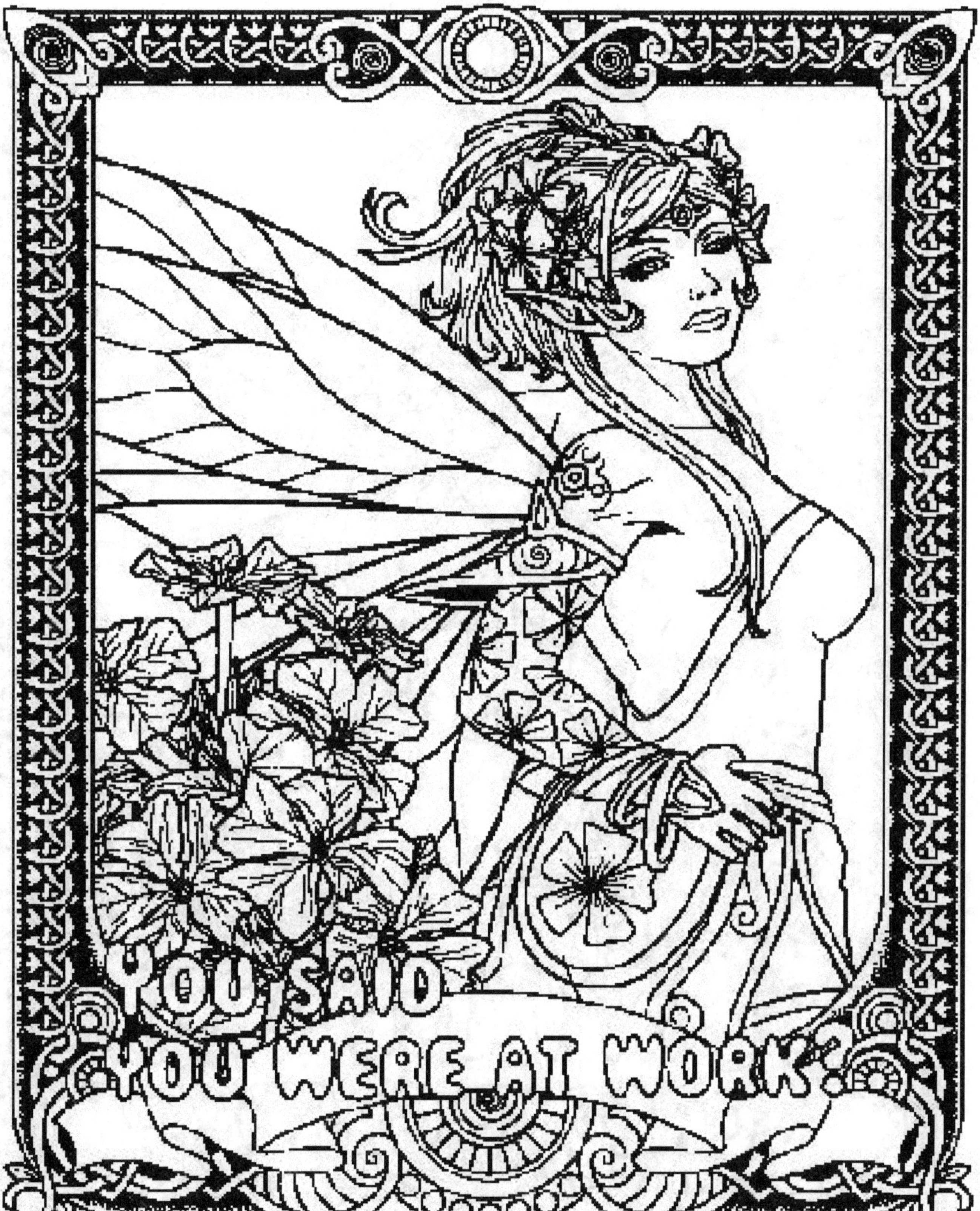
YOU SAID
YOU WERE AT WORK?

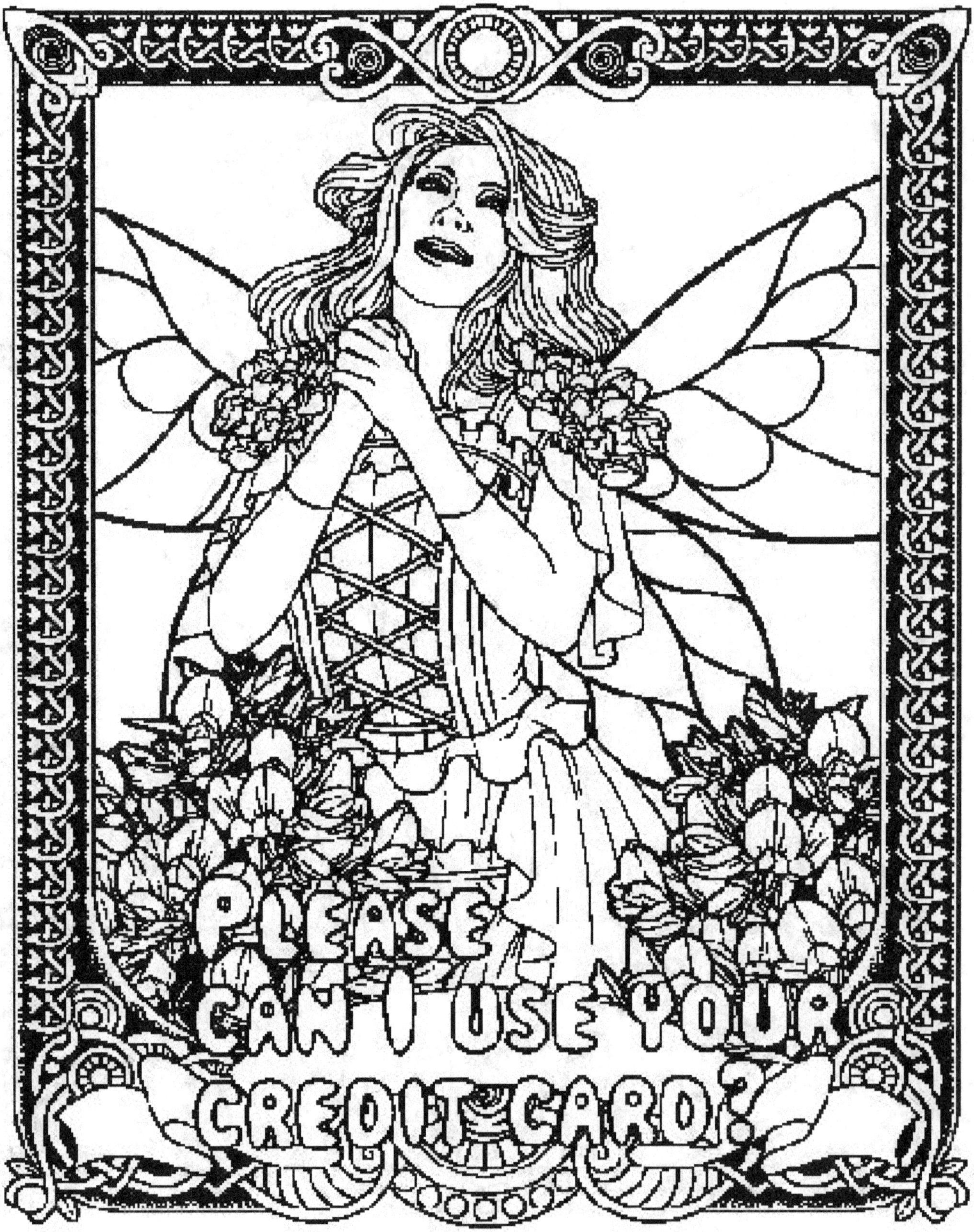
PLEASE,
CAN I USE YOUR
CREDIT CARD?

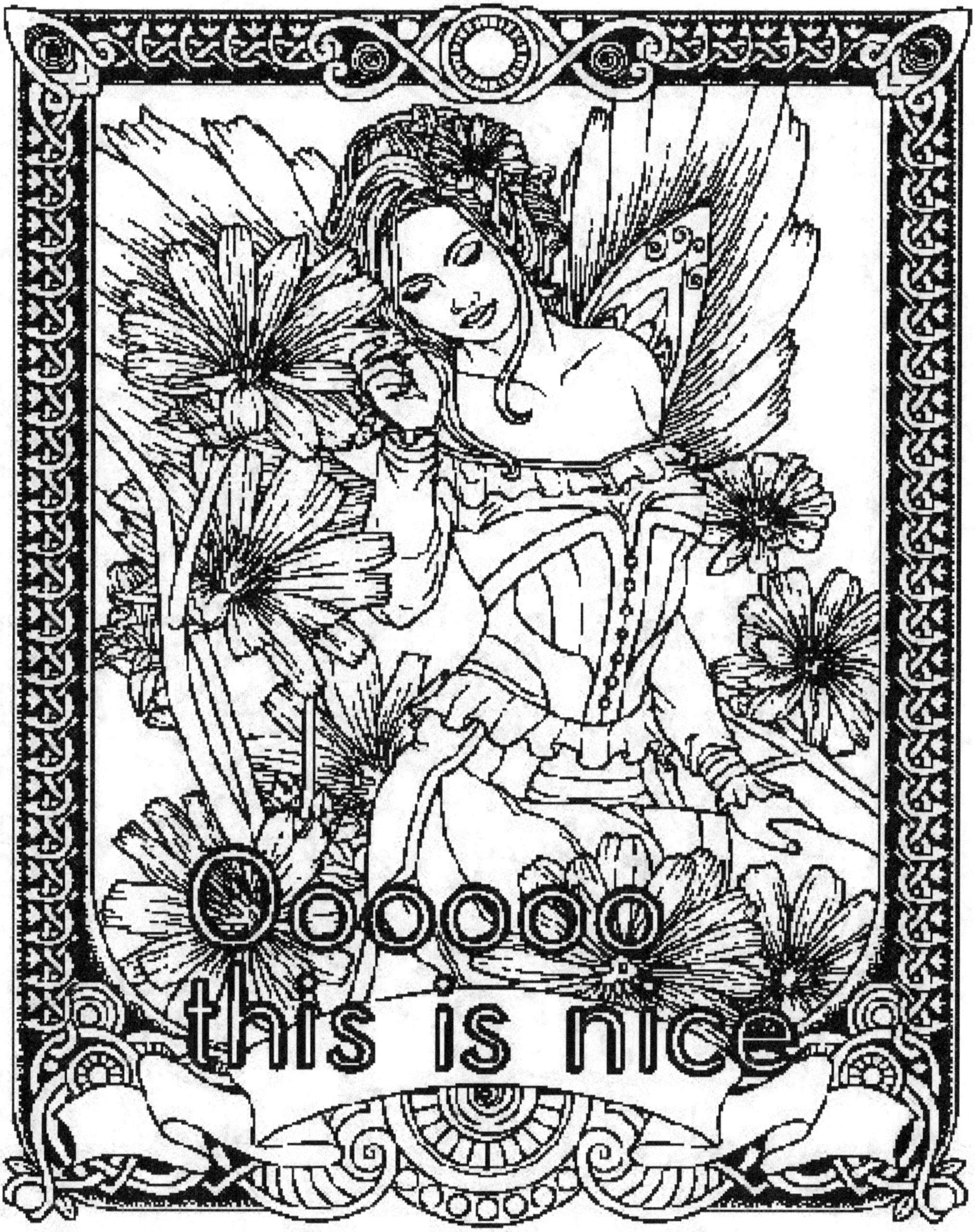
Oooooo
this is nice

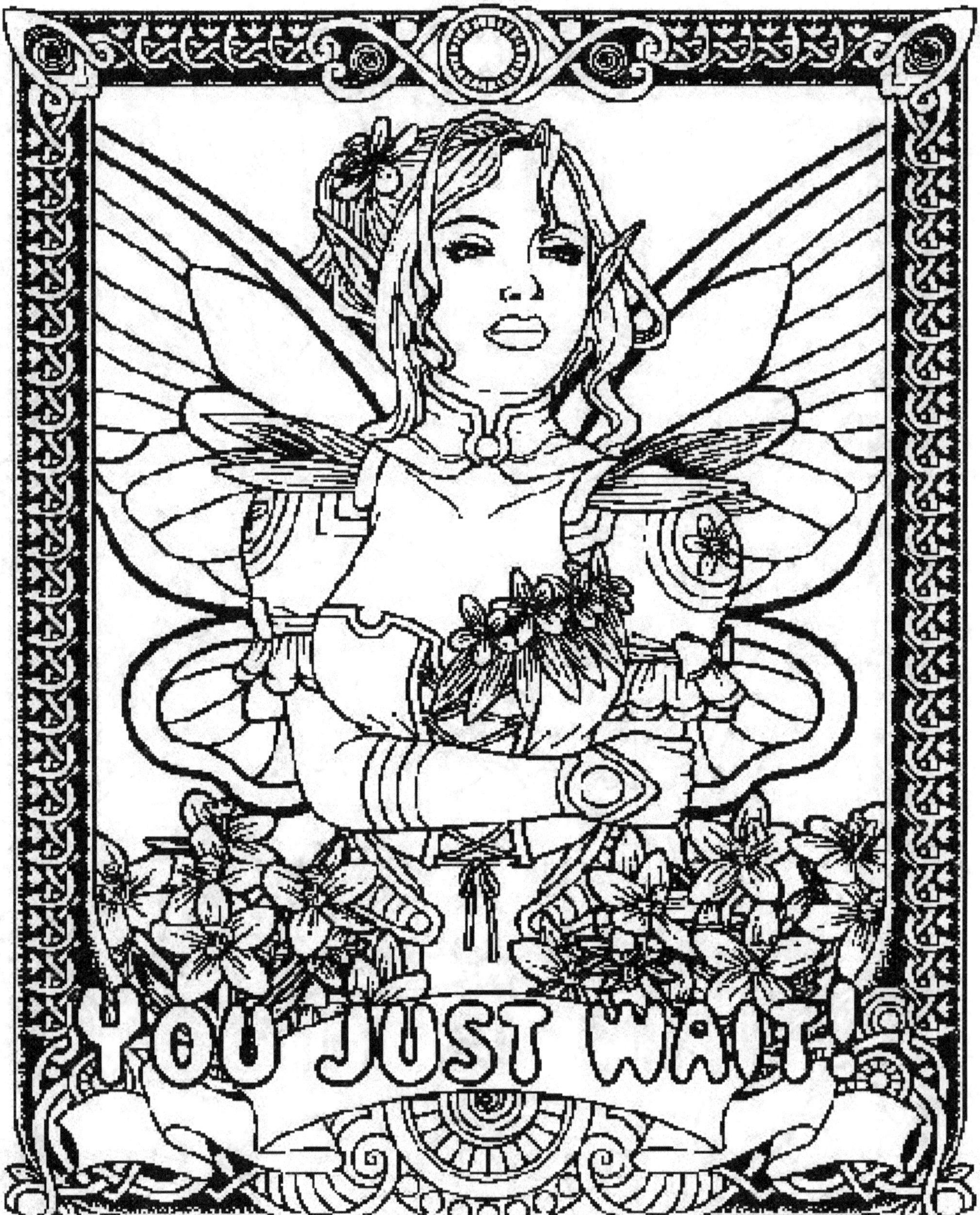
YOU JUST WAIT!

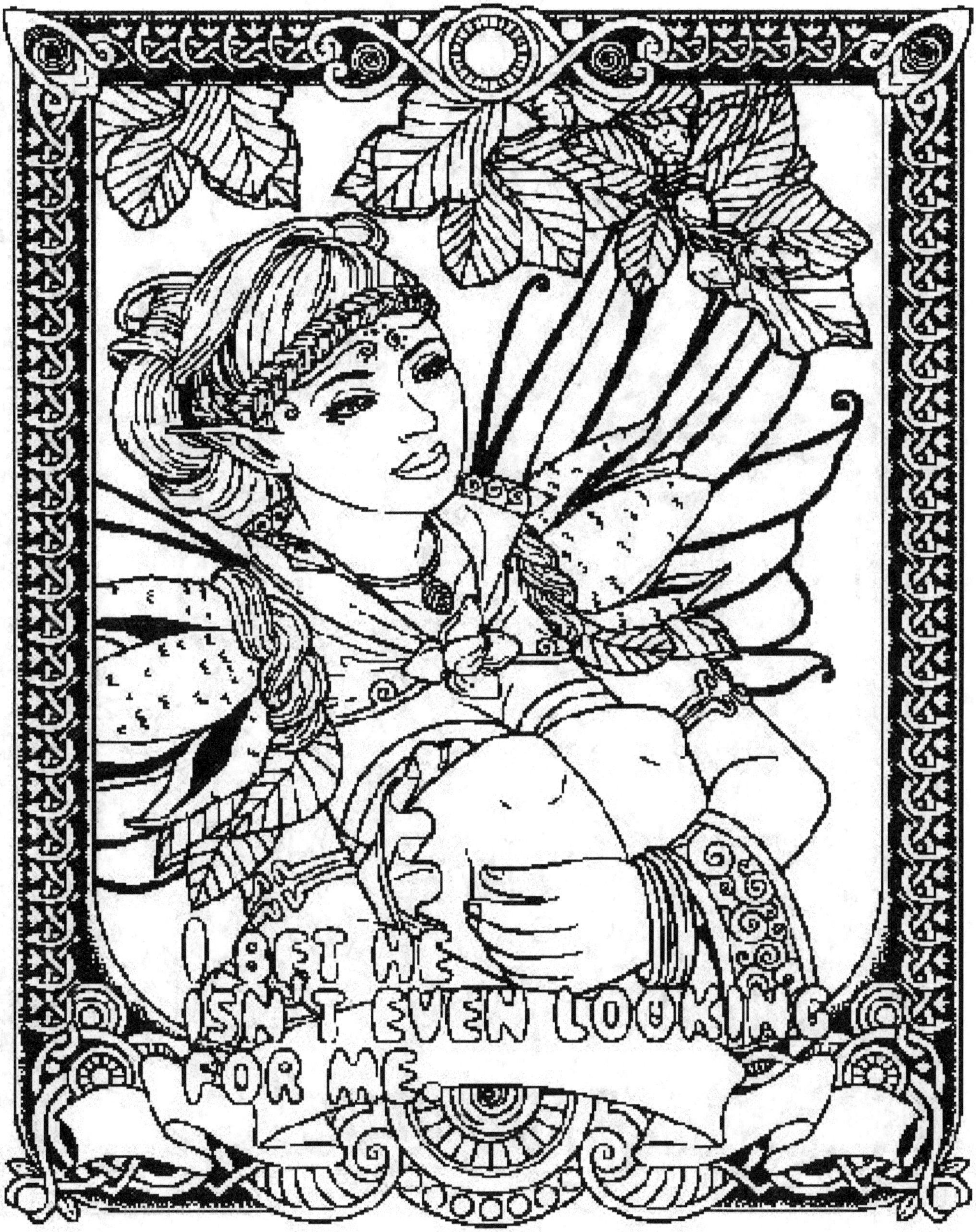
I BET HE
ISN'T EVEN LOOKING
FOR ME.

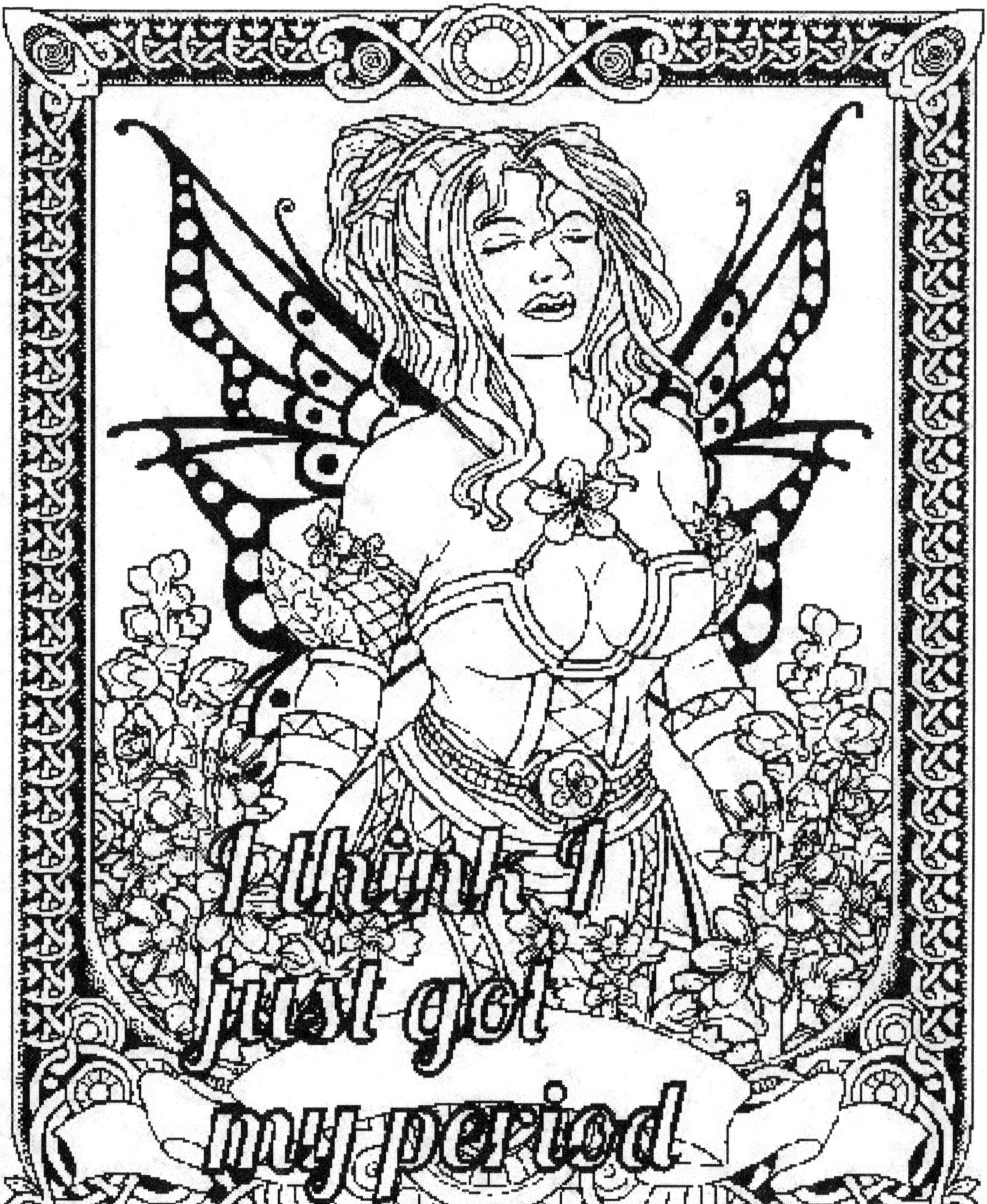
I think I
just got
my period

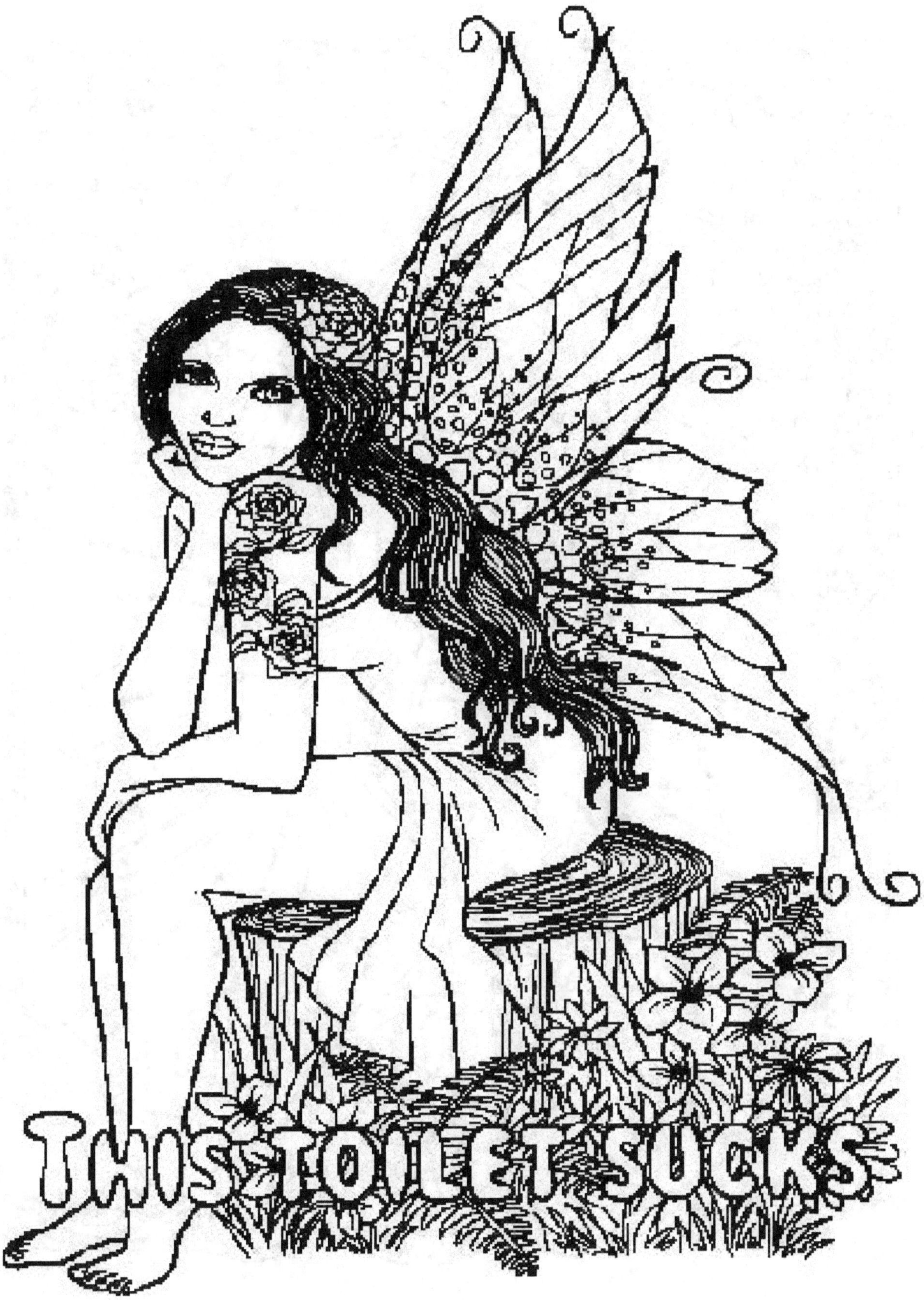
THIS TOILET SUCKS

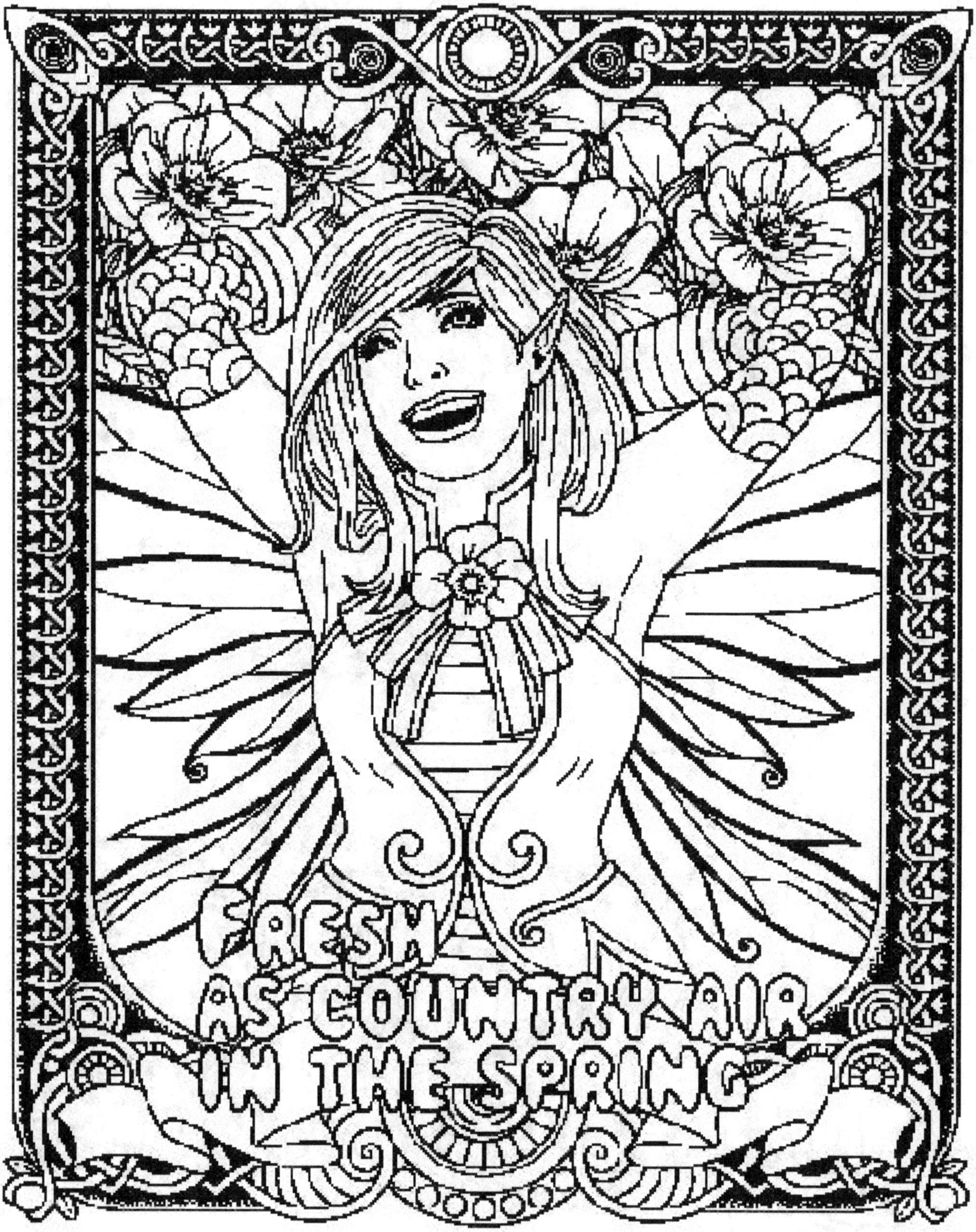
FRESH
AS COUNTRY AIR
IN THE SPRING

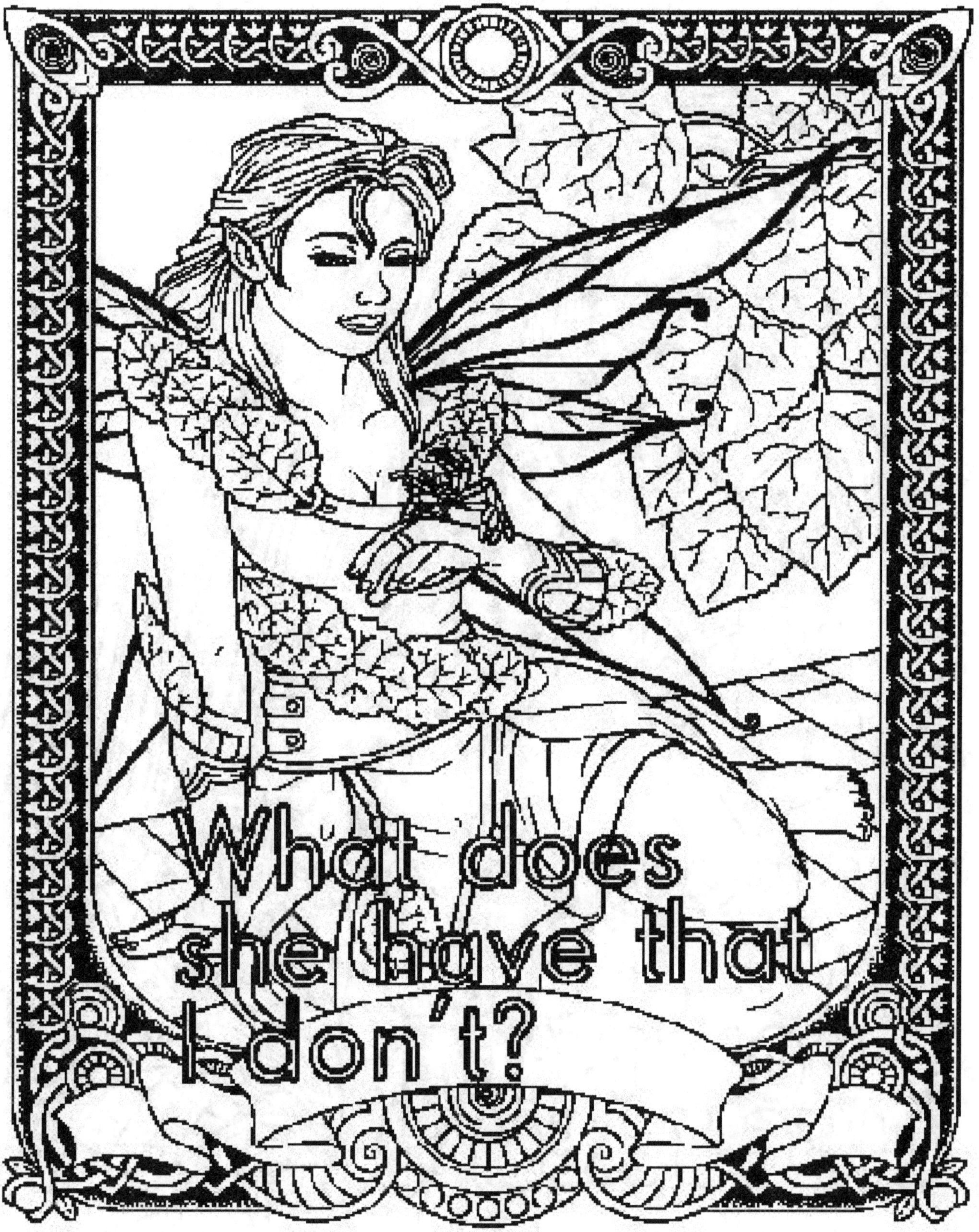
What does
she have that
I don't?

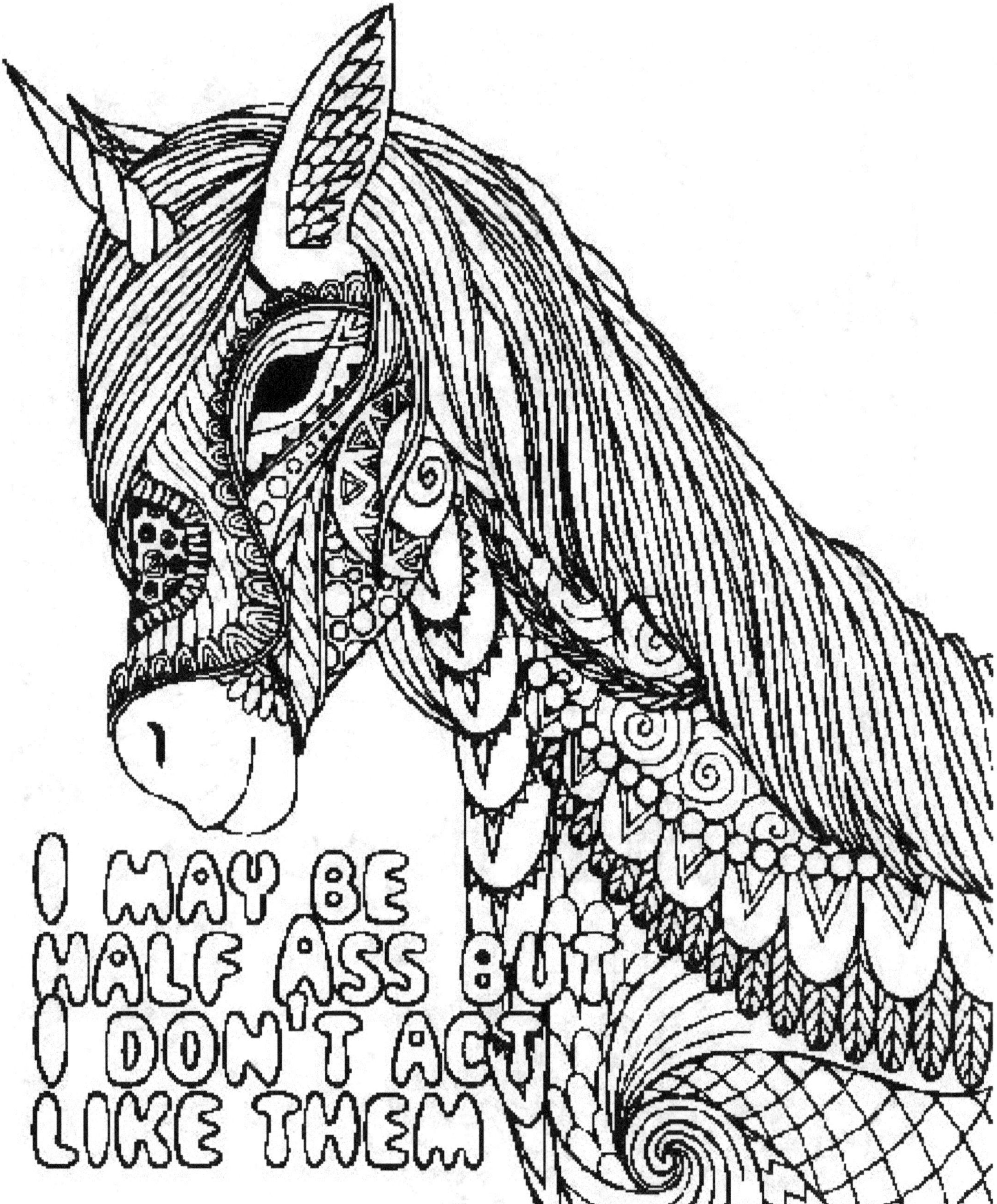
I MAY BE
HALF ASS BUT
I DON'T ACT
LIKE THEM

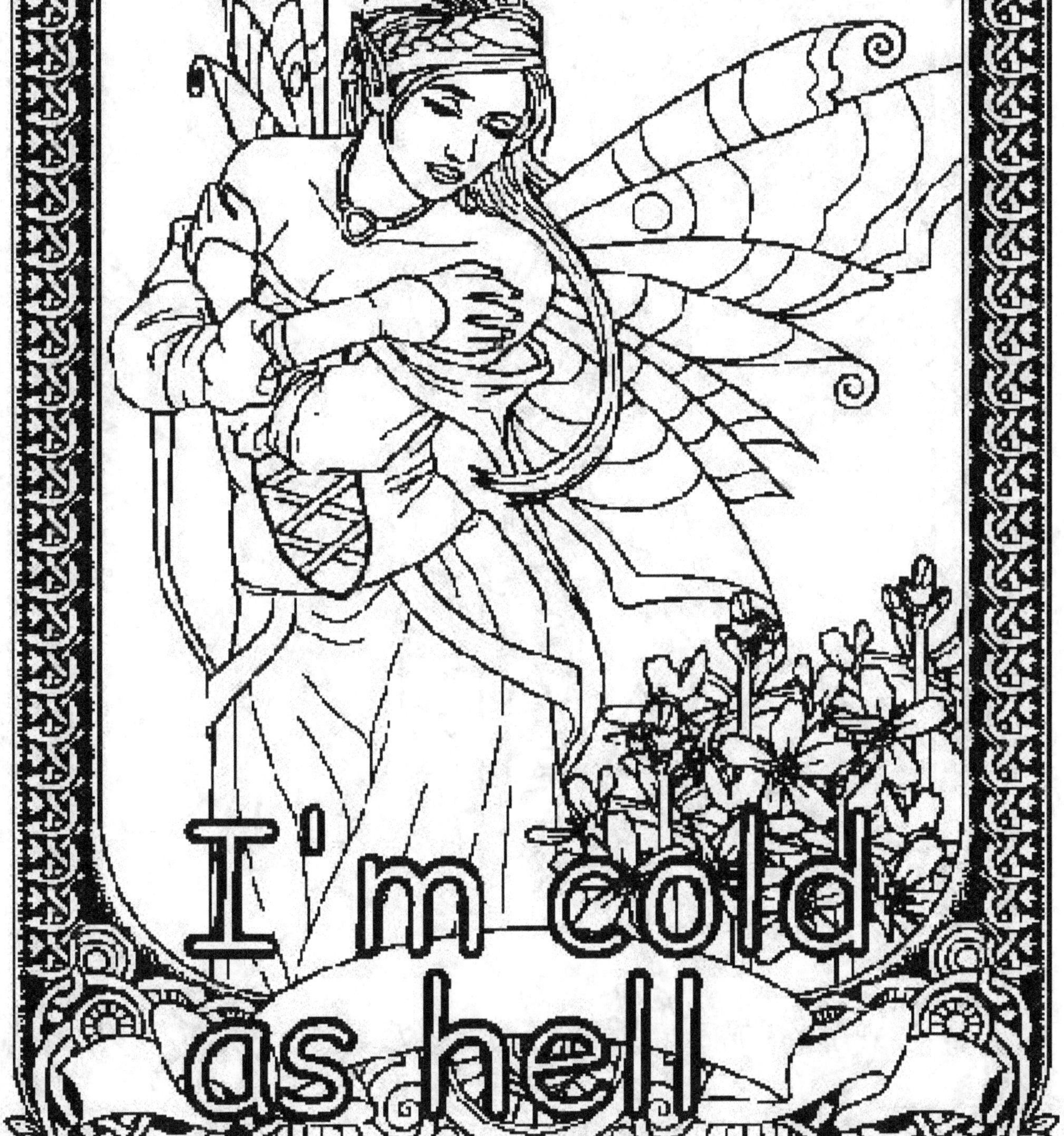
I'm cold
as hell

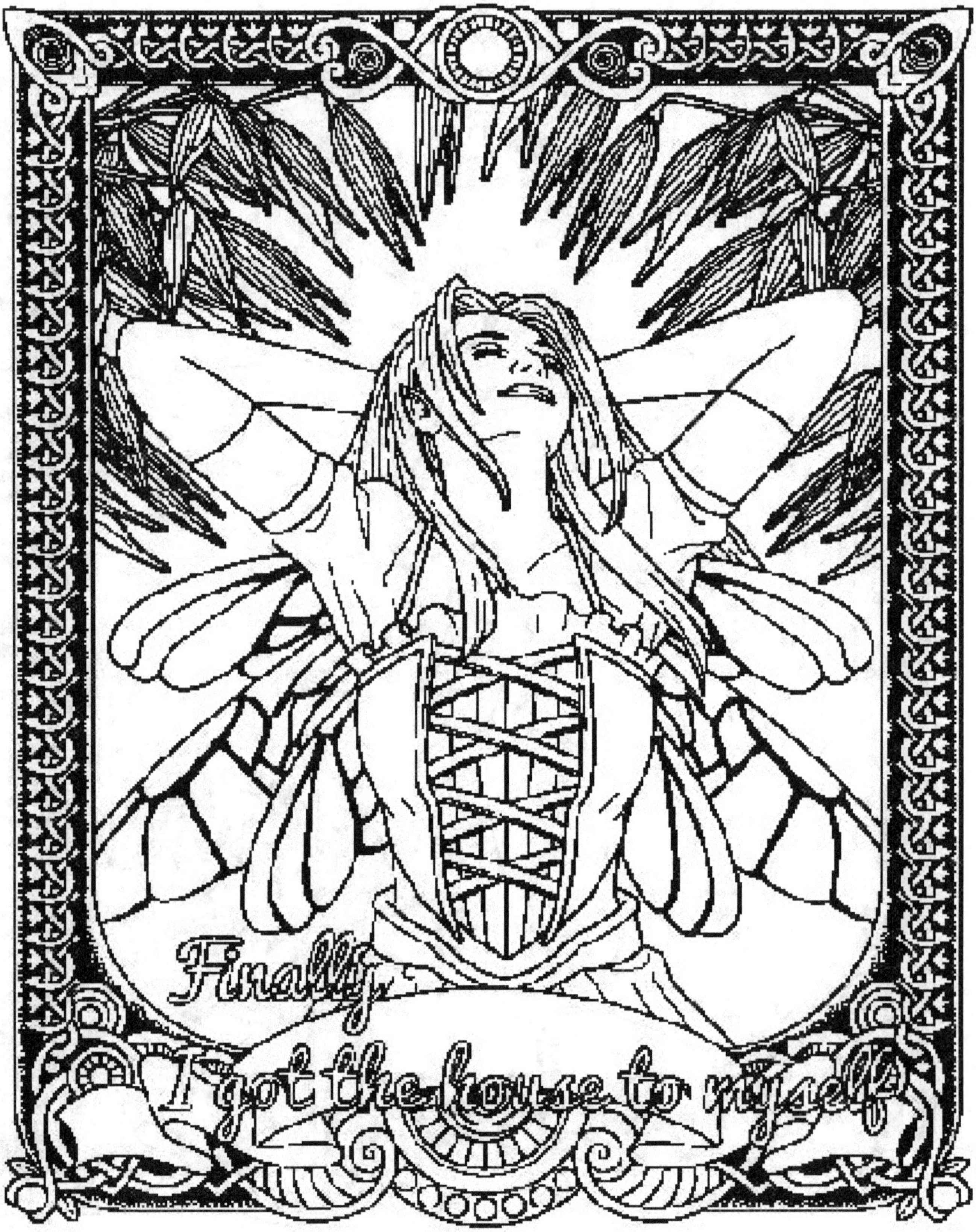
Finally
I got the house to myself

I WISH I HAD WINGS

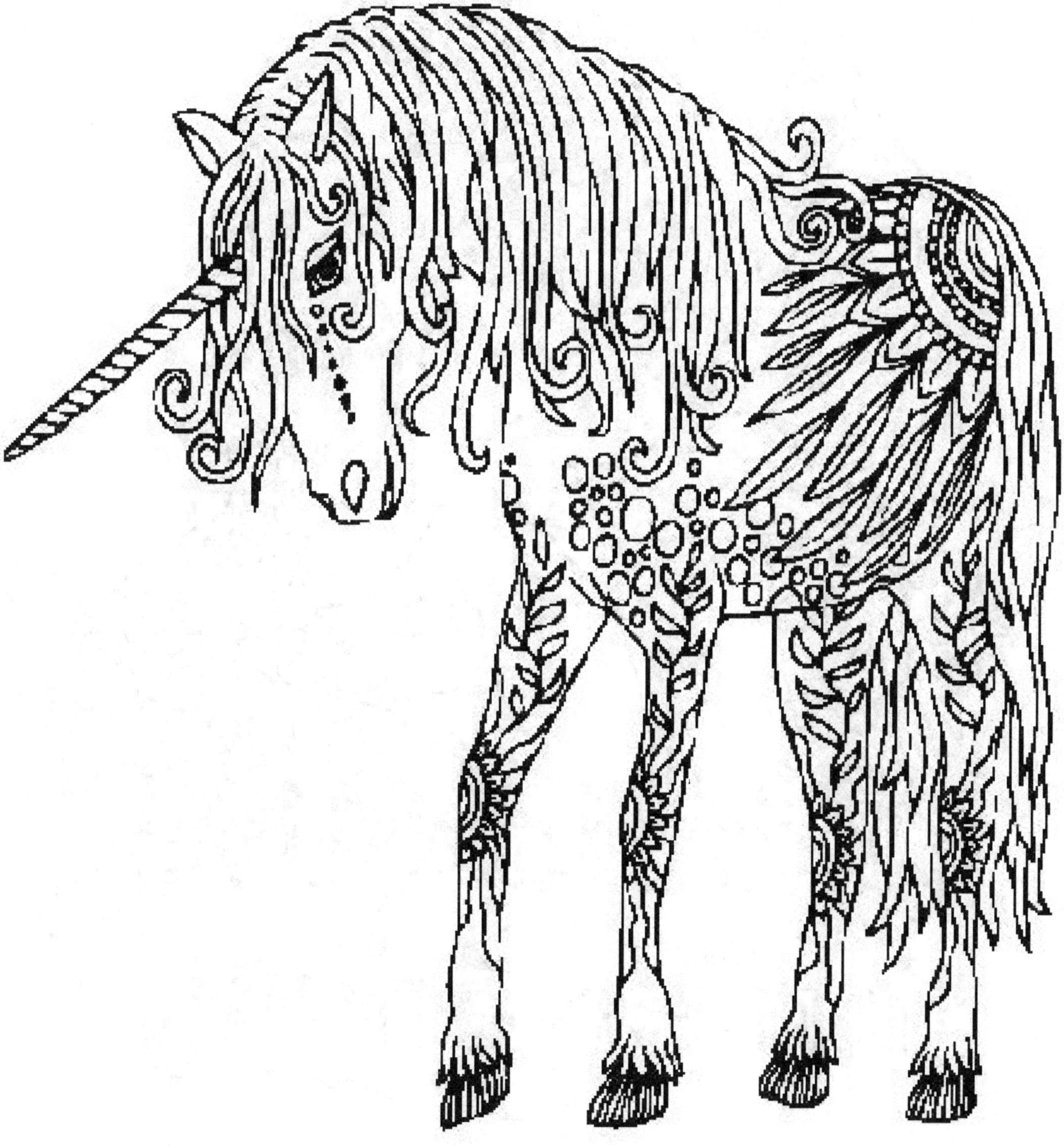

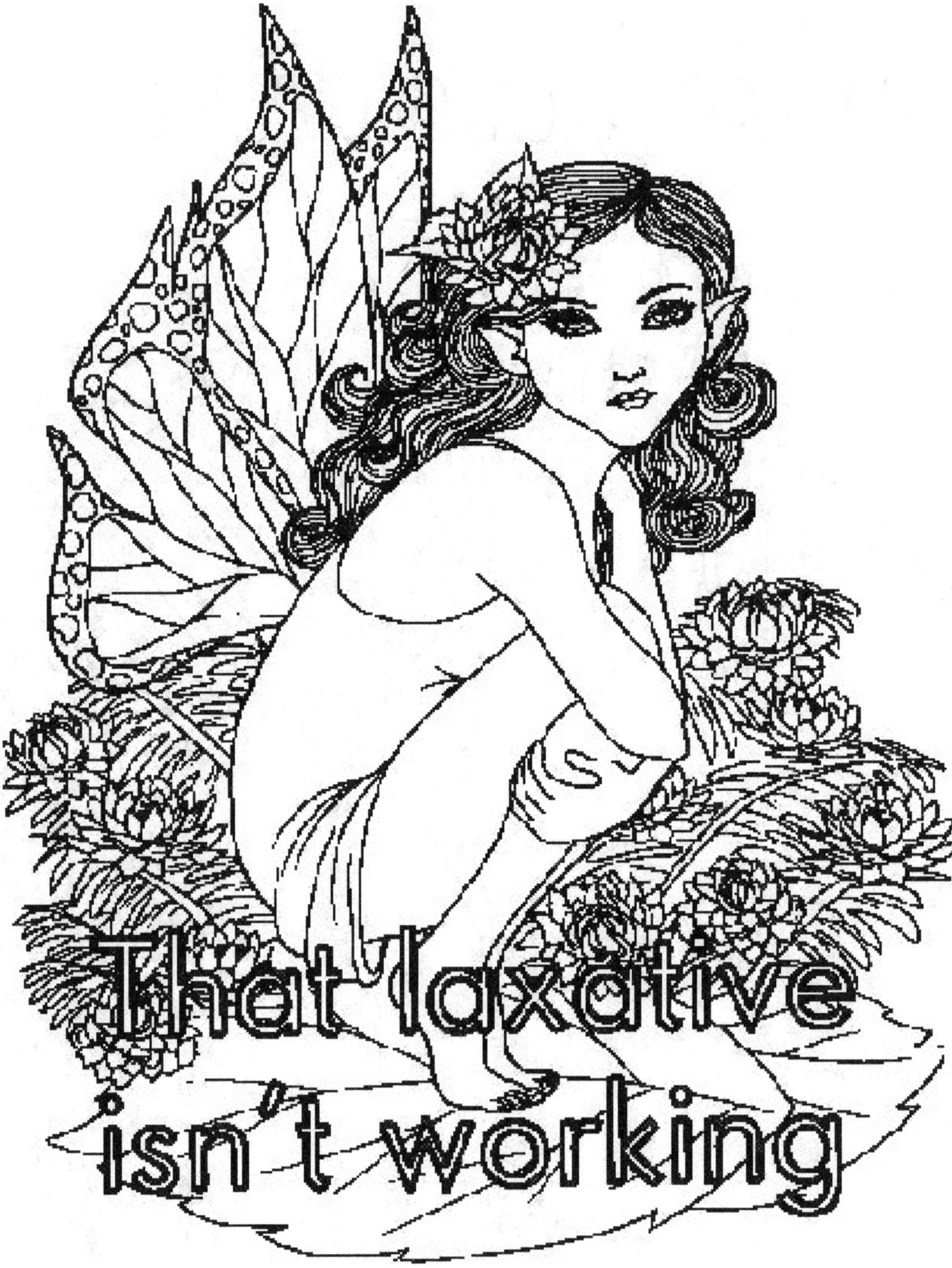
That laxative
isn't working

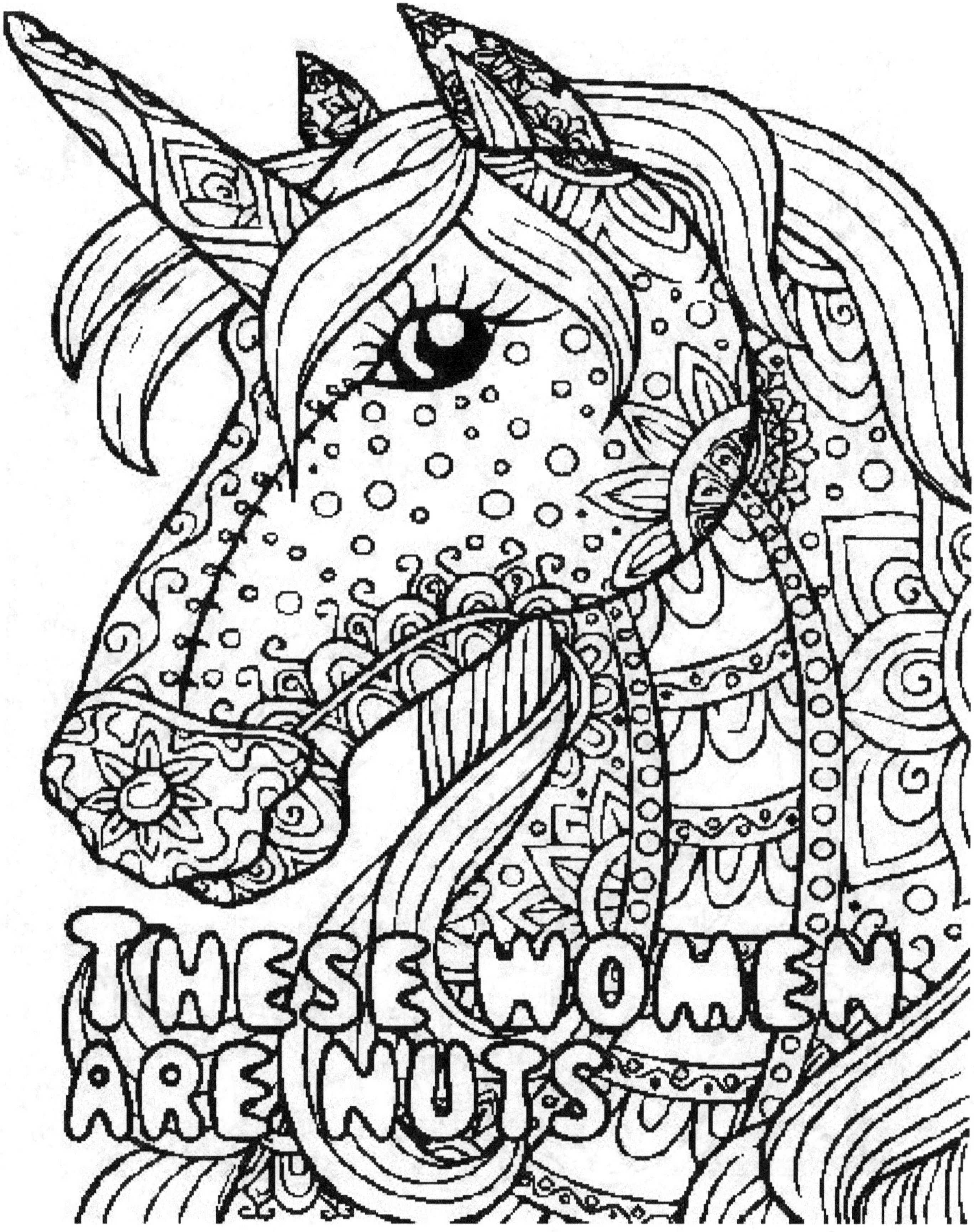
THESE WOMEN
ARE NUTS

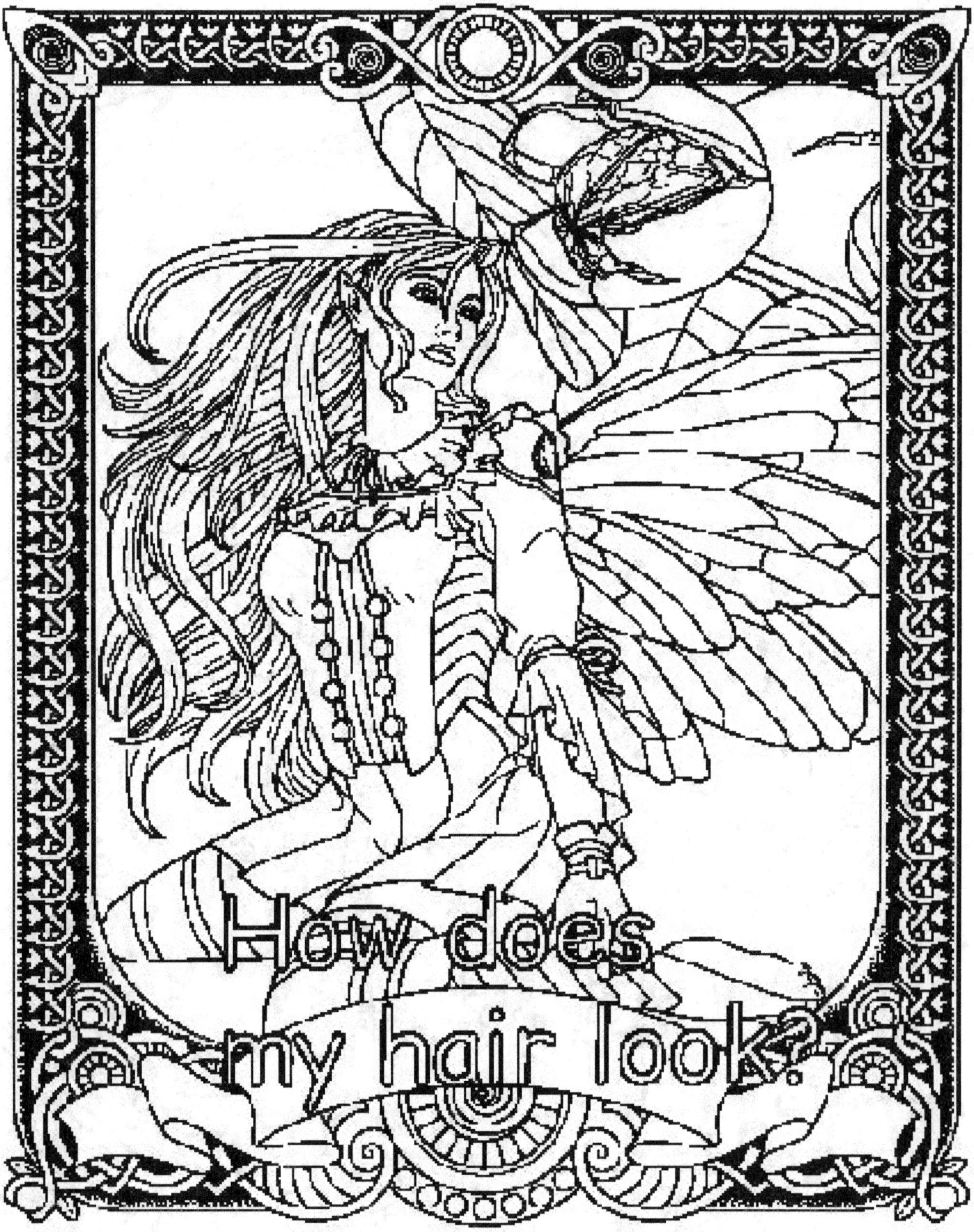
How does
my hair look?

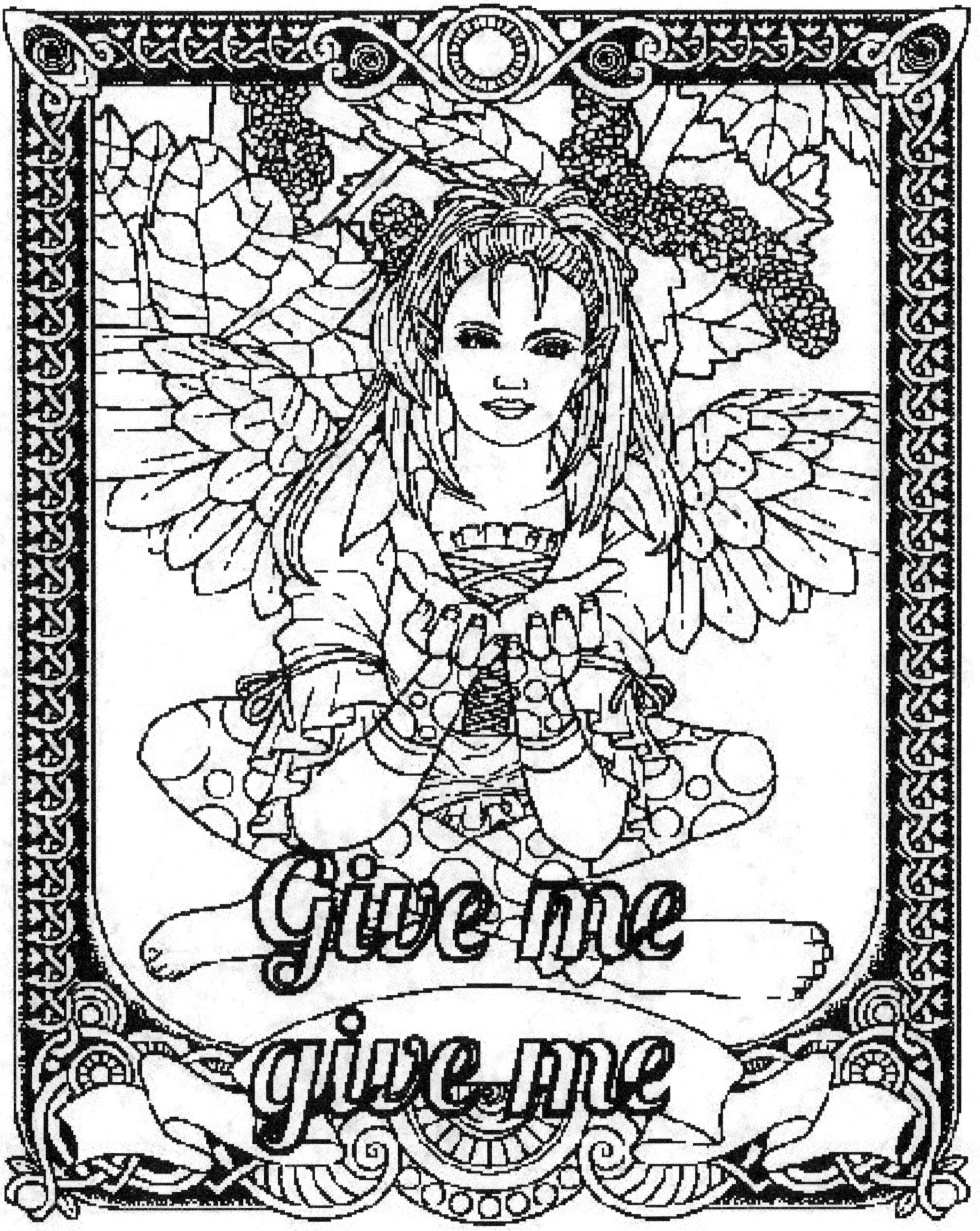
Give me
give me

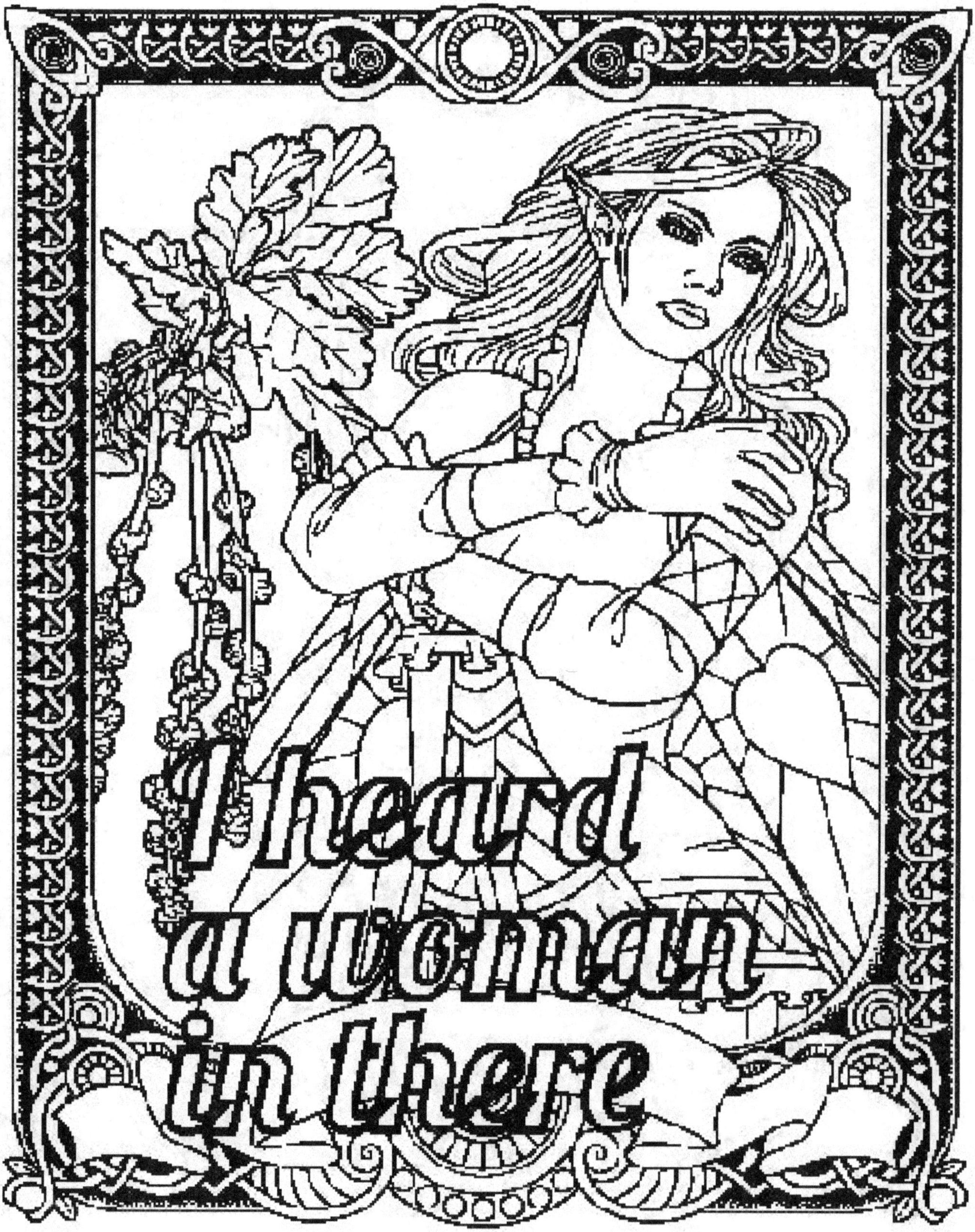
I heard
a woman
in there

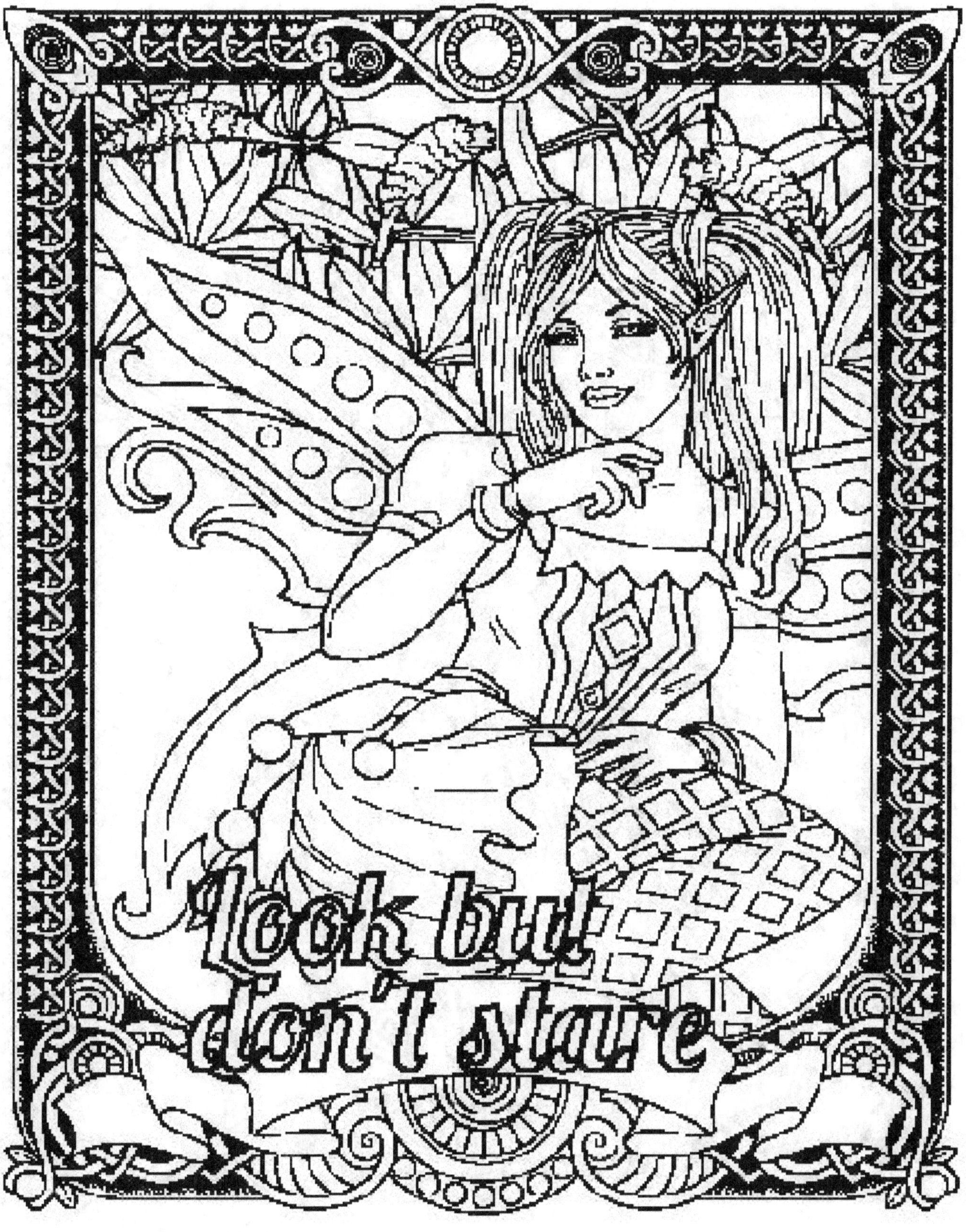
look but
don't stare

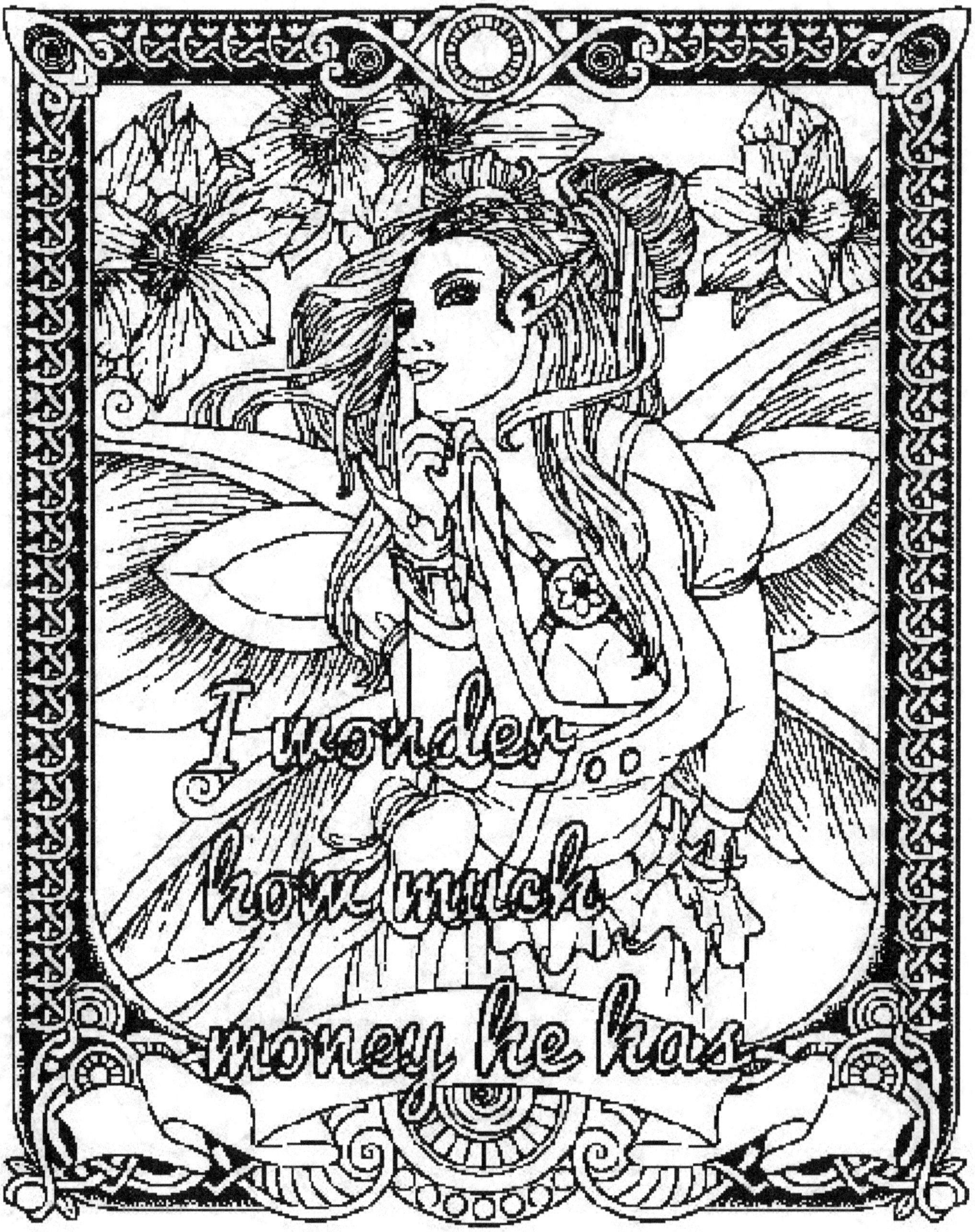
I wonder...
how much
money he has

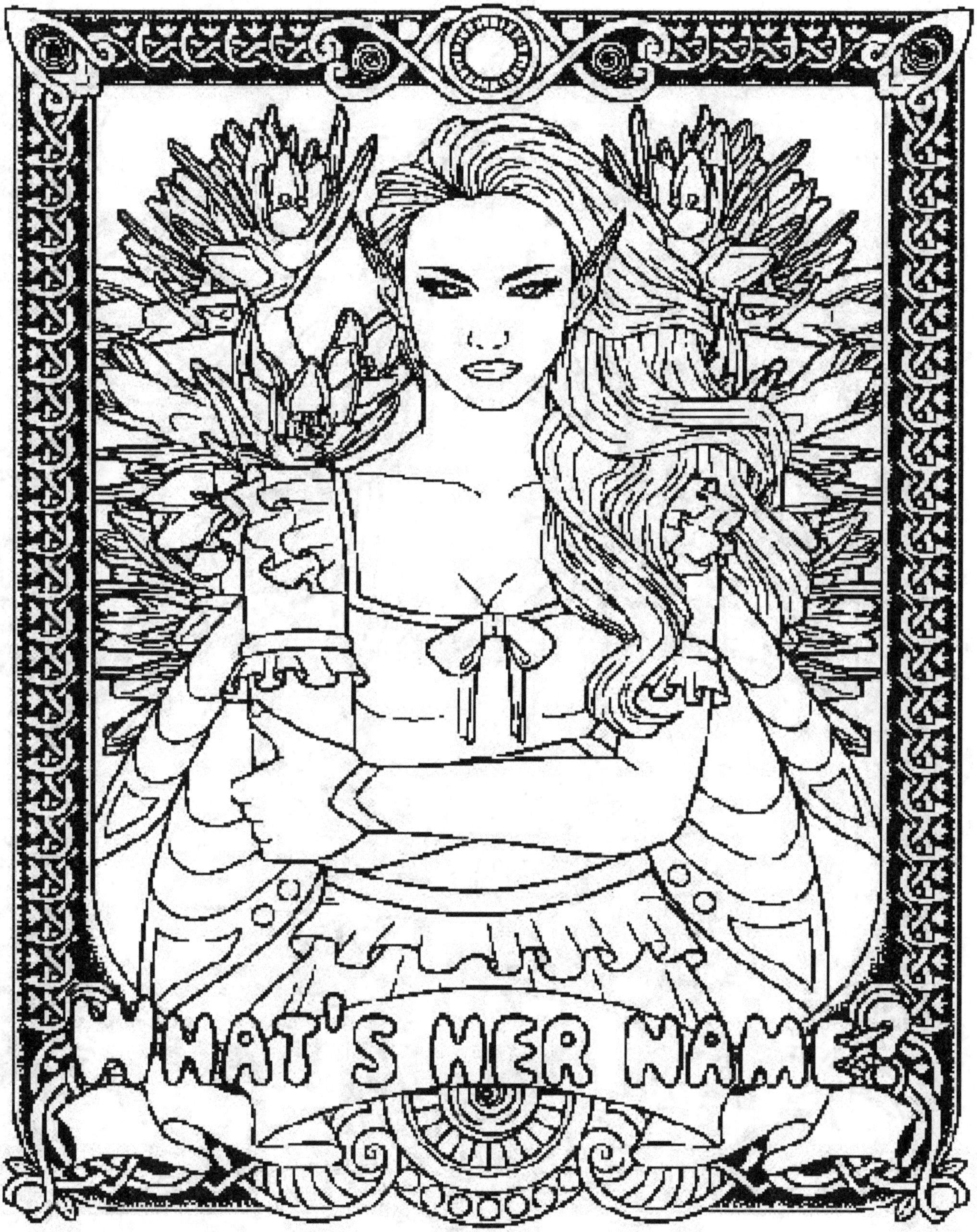
WHAT'S HER NAME?

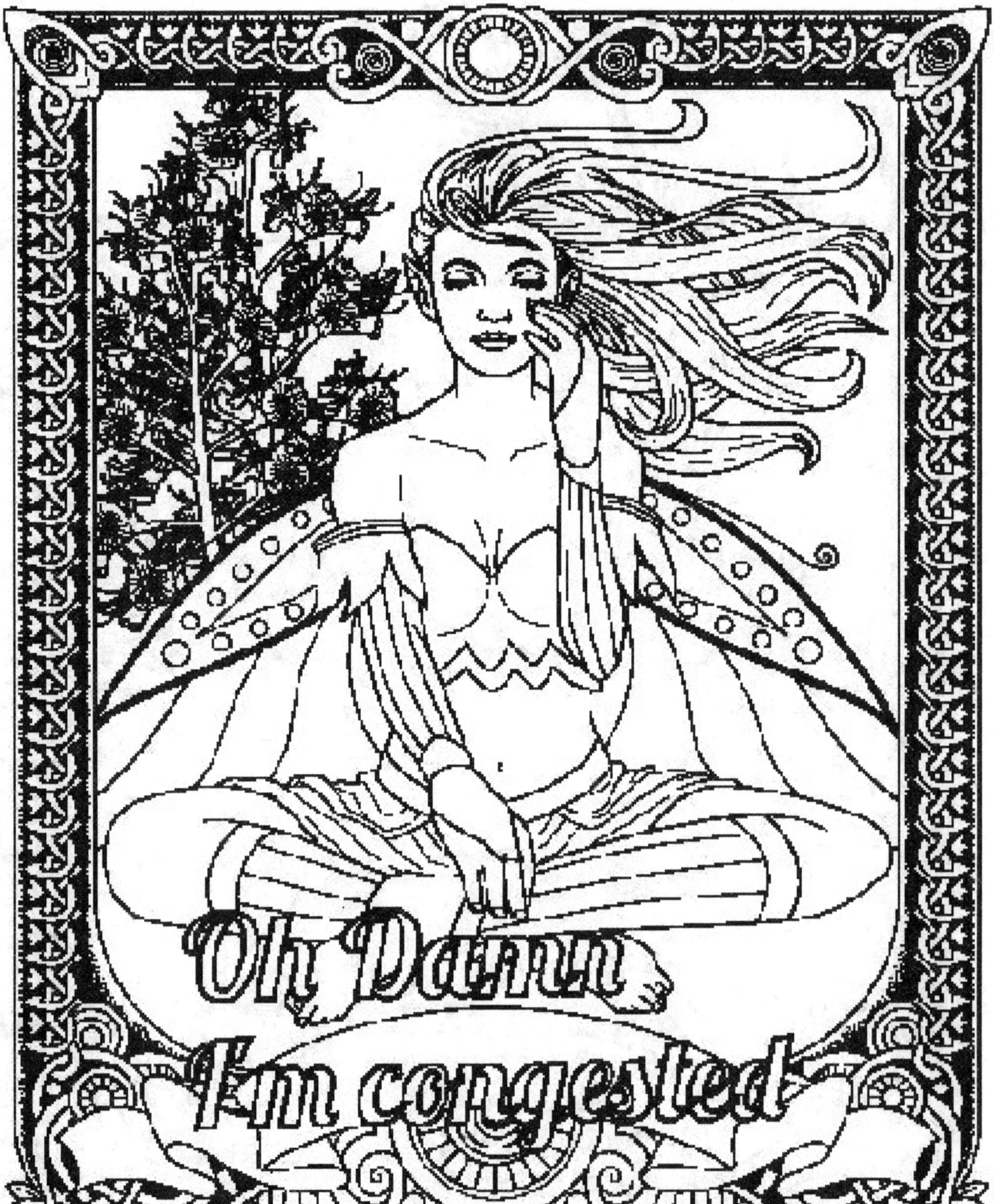
Oh Damn
I'm congested

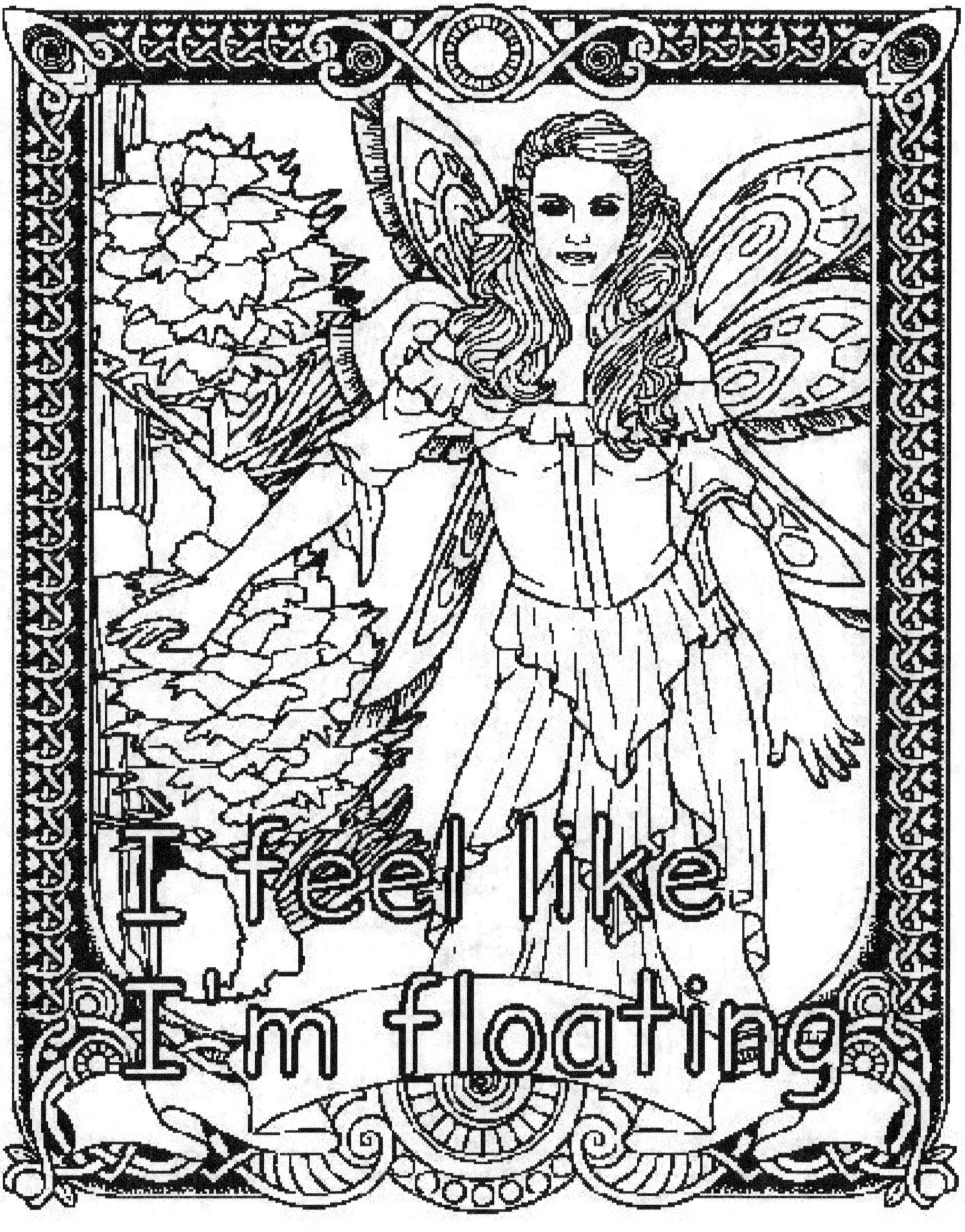
I feel like
I'm floating

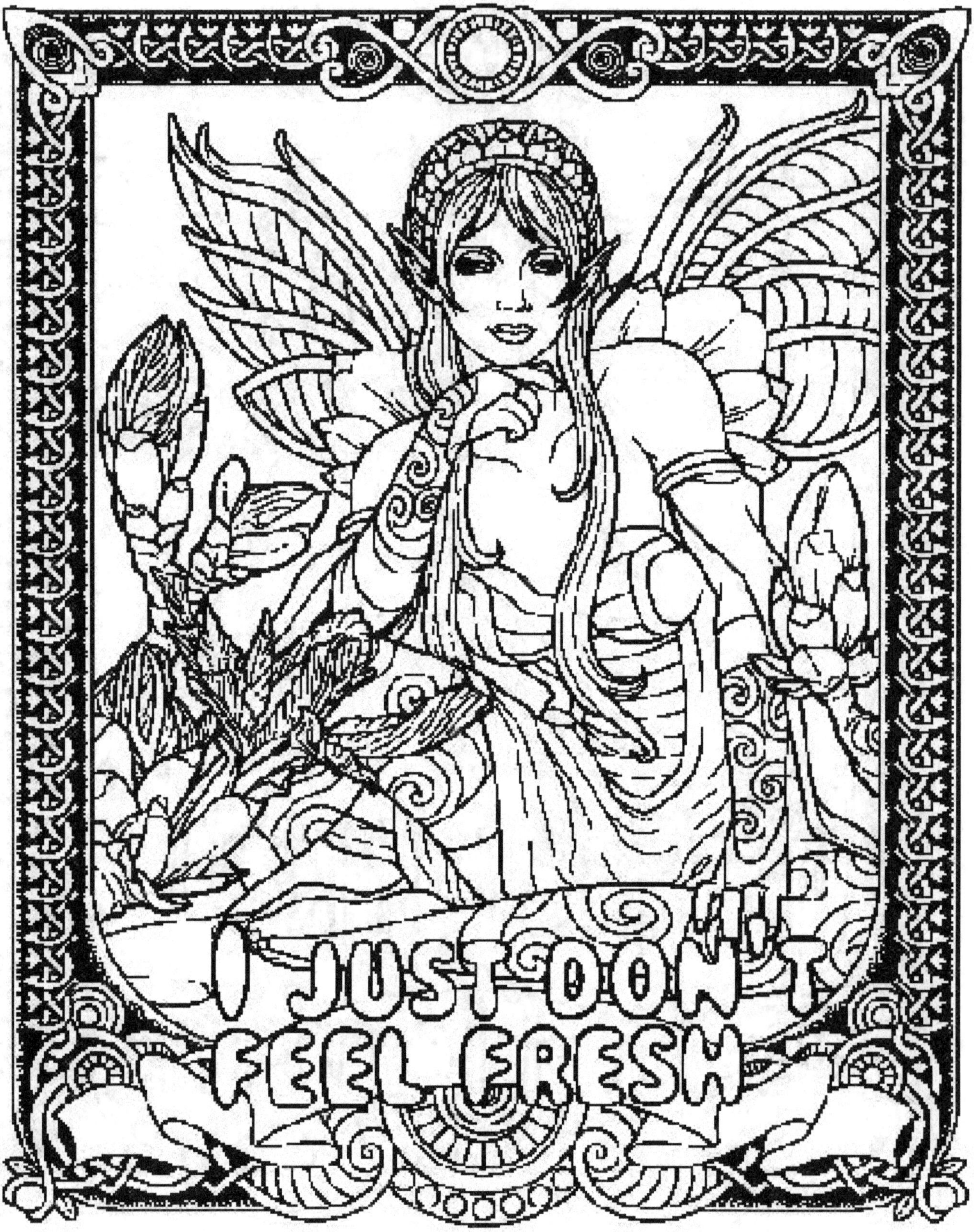
I JUST DON'T
FEEL FRESH

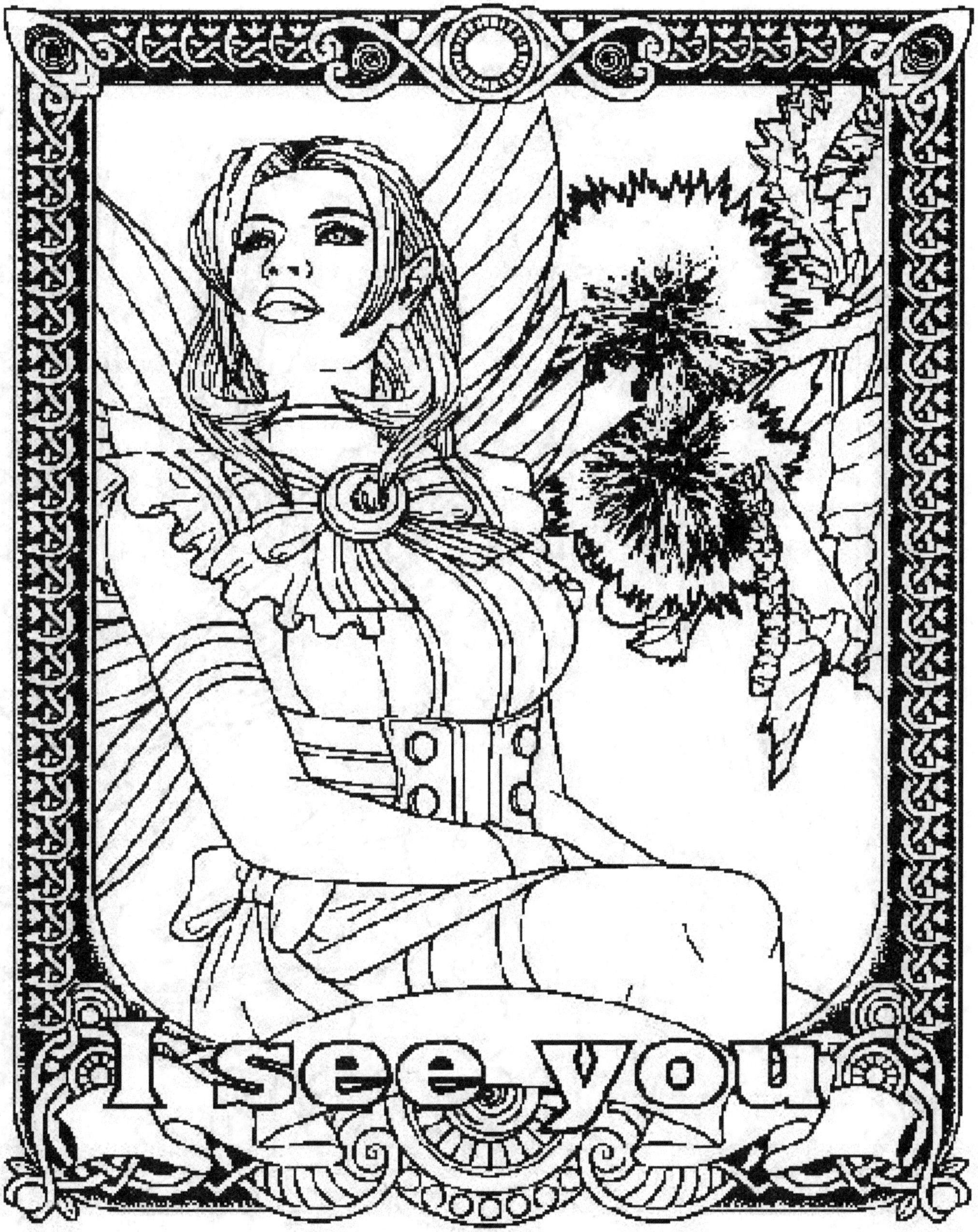
I see you

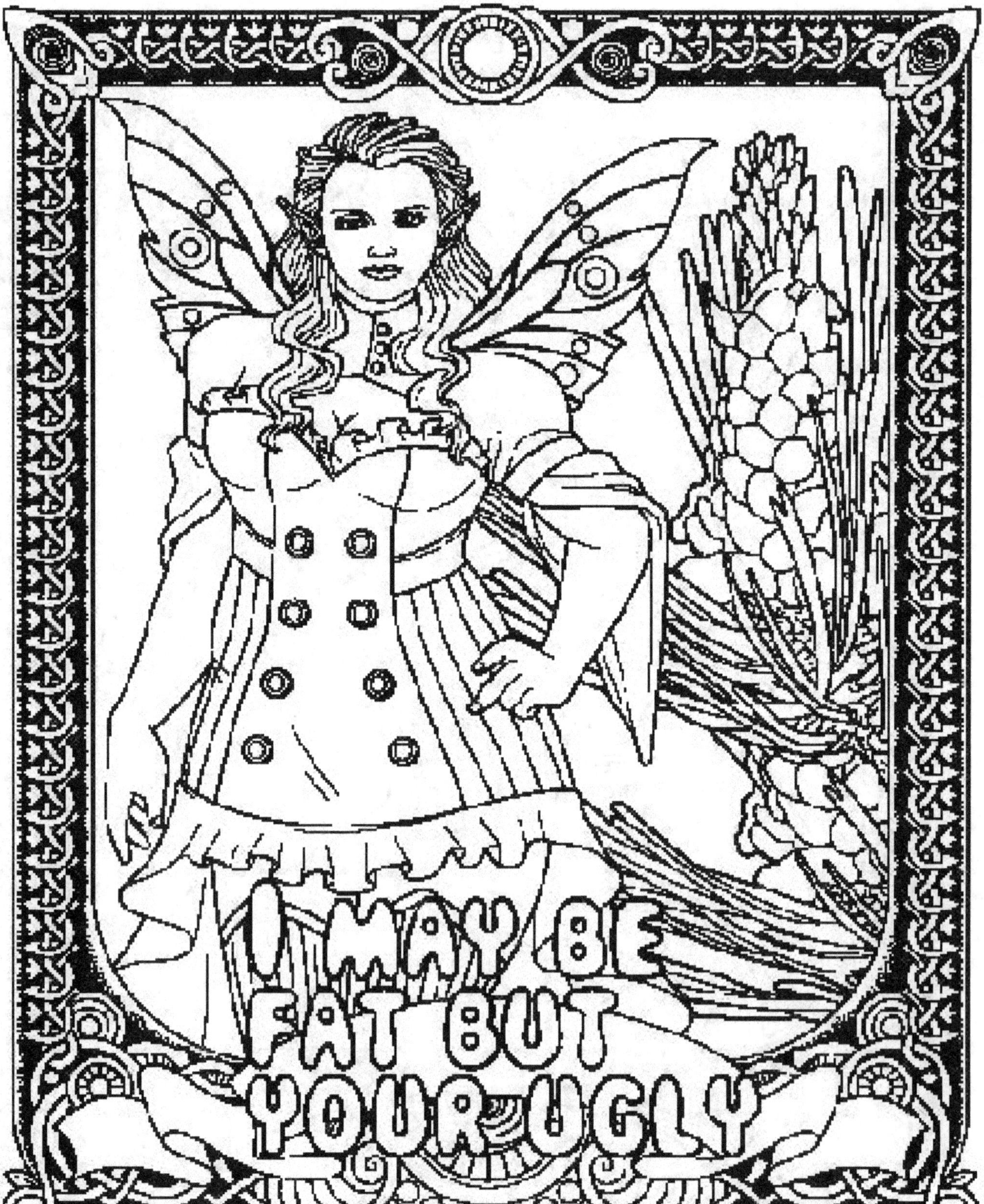
I MAY BE
FAT BUT
YOUR UGLY

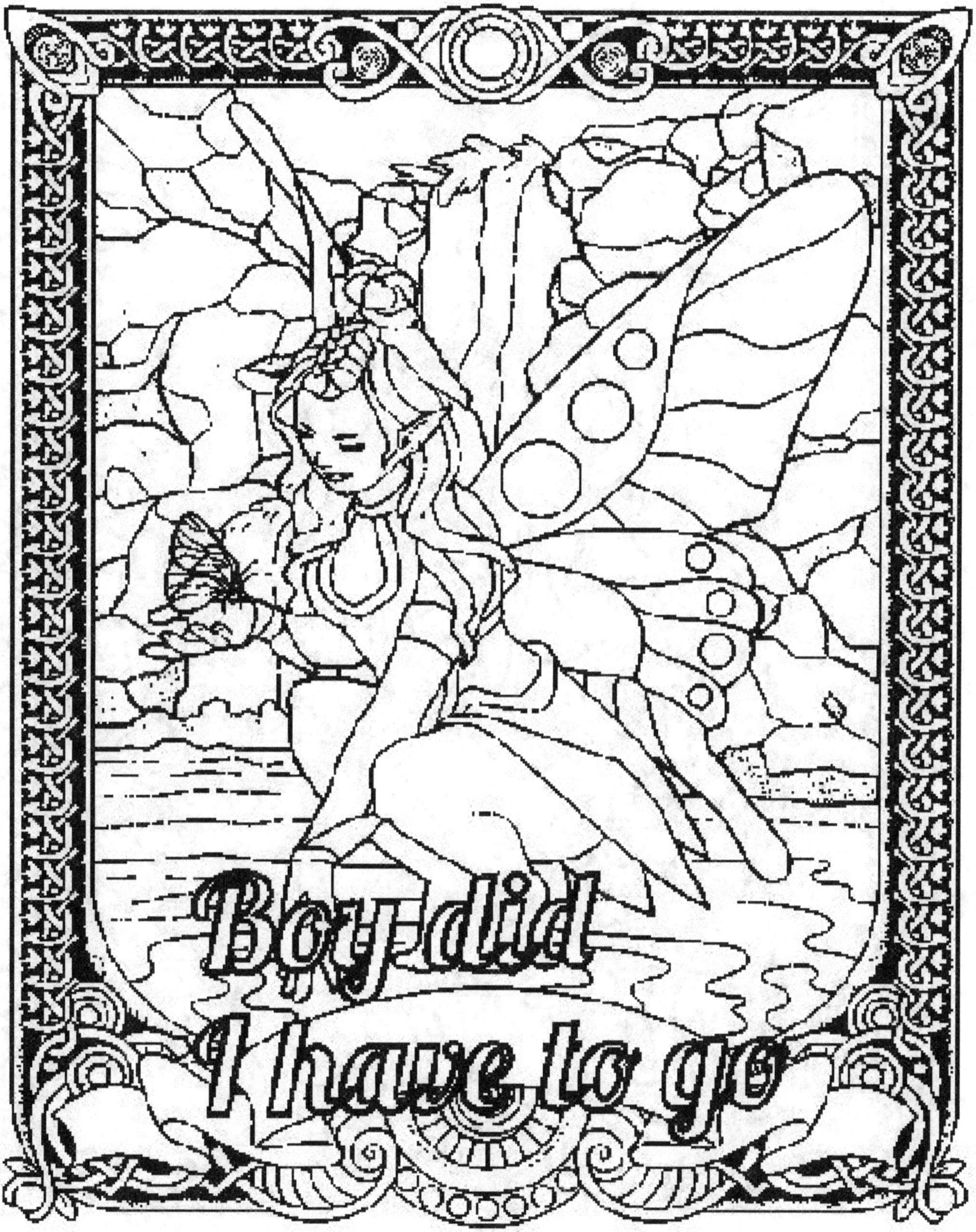
Boy did
I have to go

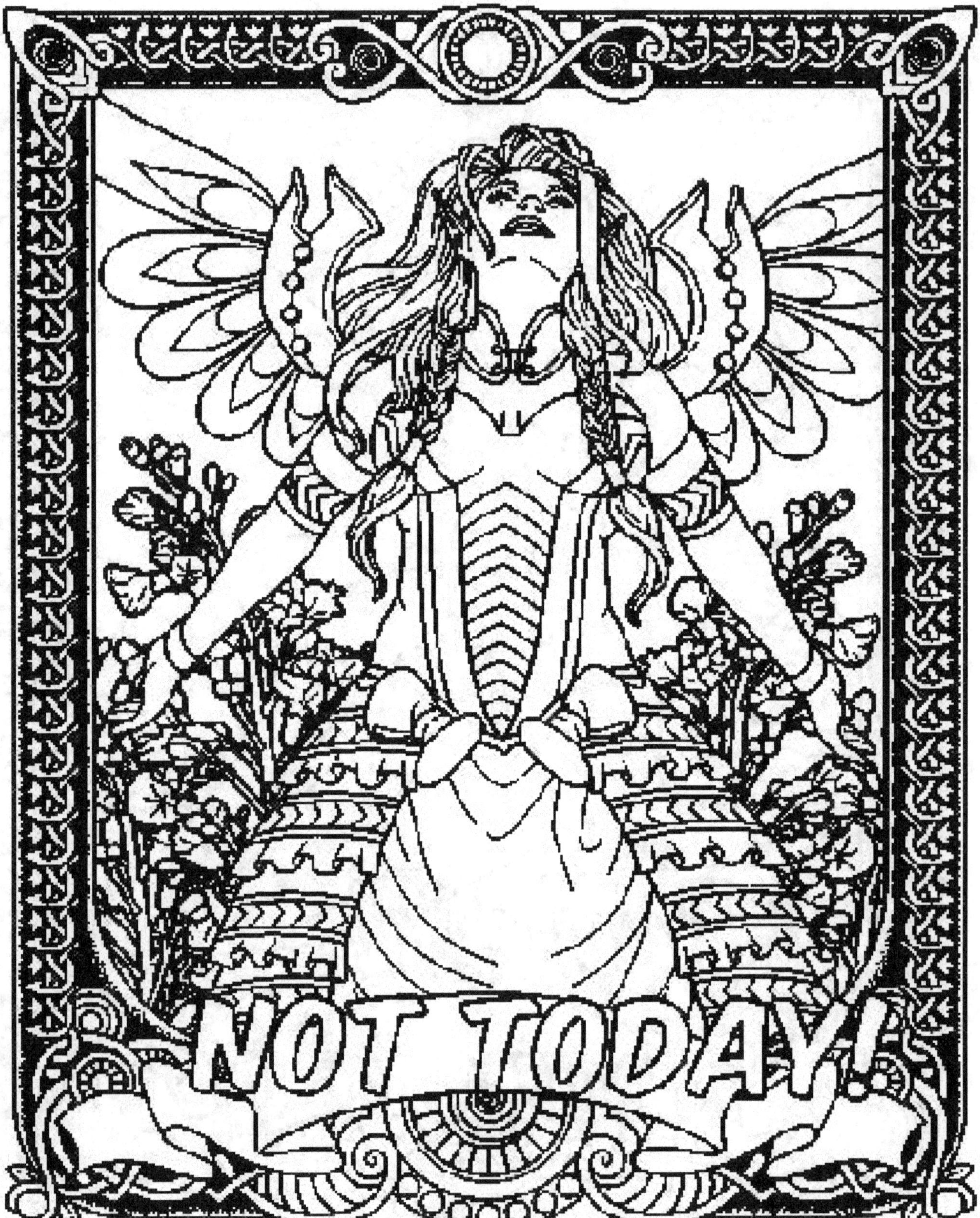
NOT TODAY!

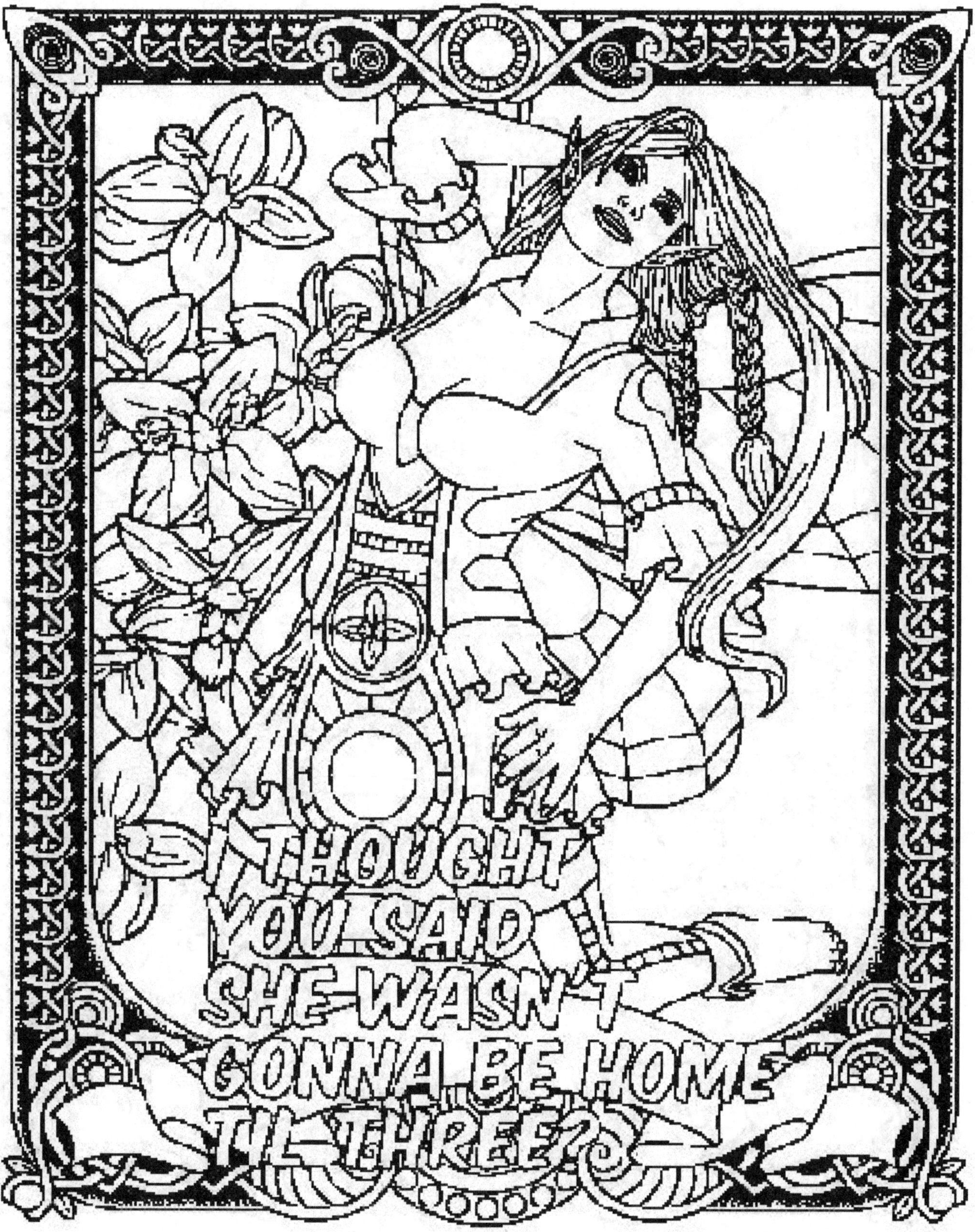
I THOUGHT
YOU SAID
SHE WASN'T
GONNA BE HOME
TIL THREE?

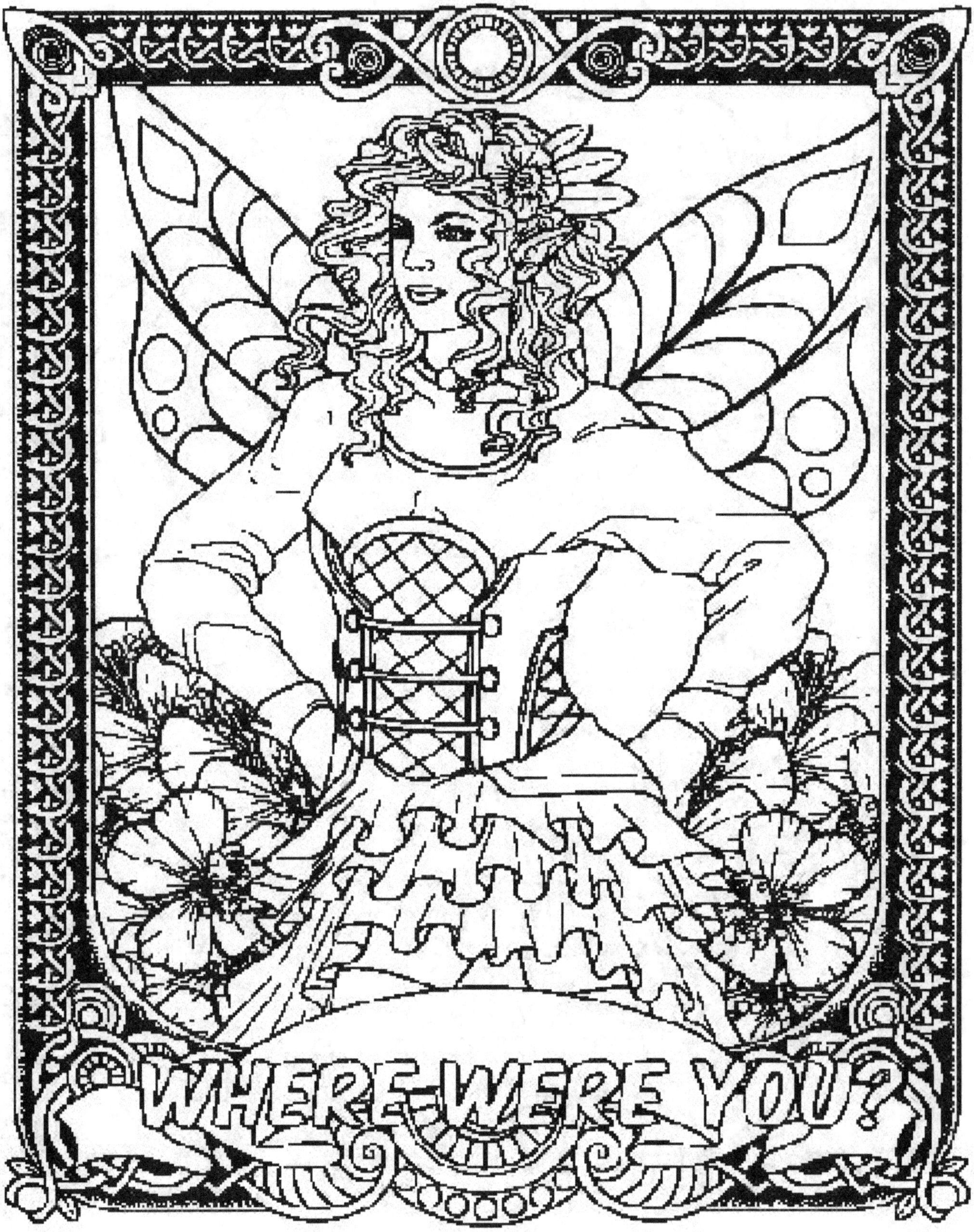
WHERE-WERE YOU?

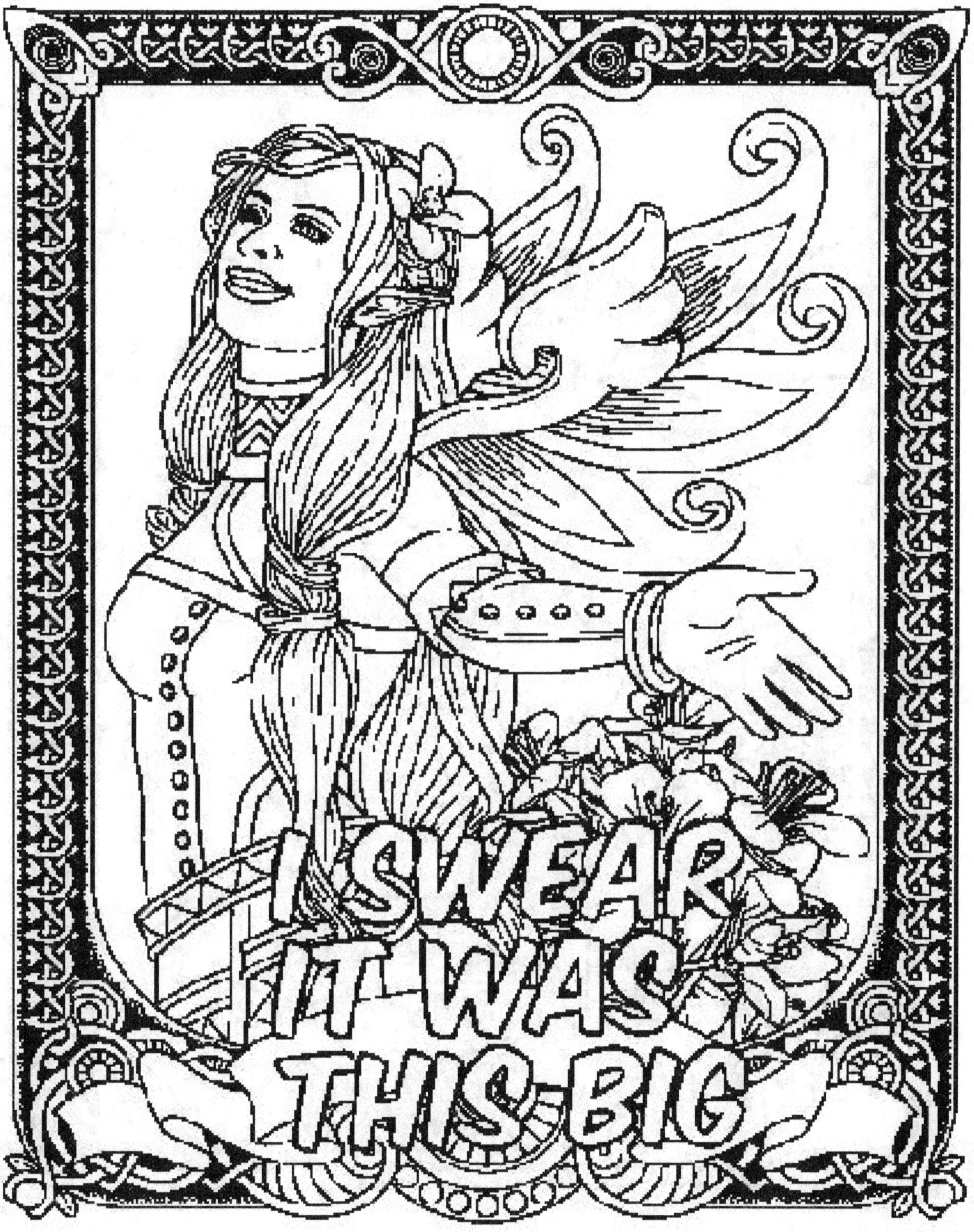
I SWEAR
IT WAS
THIS BIG

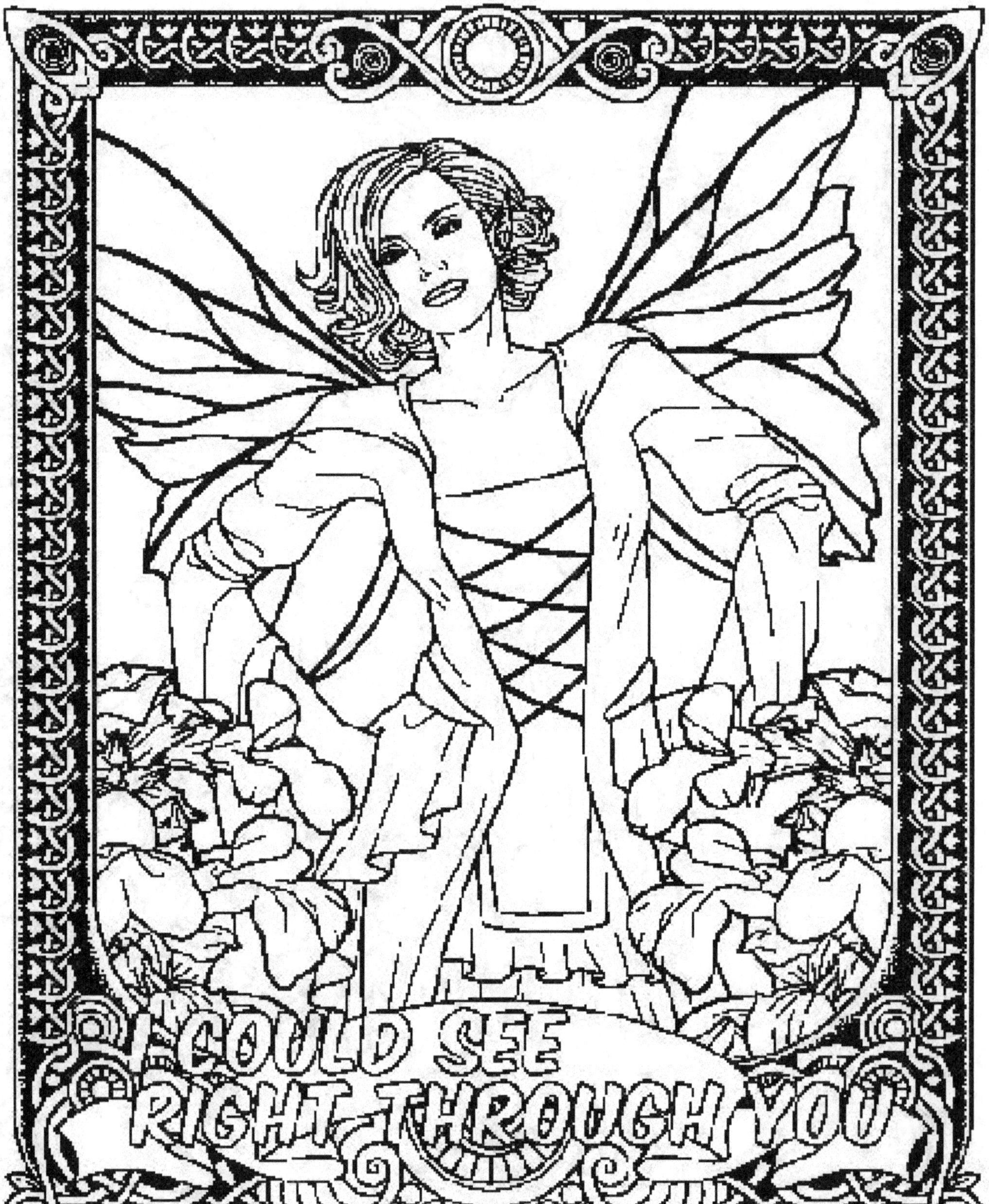
I COULD SEE
RIGHT THROUGH YOU

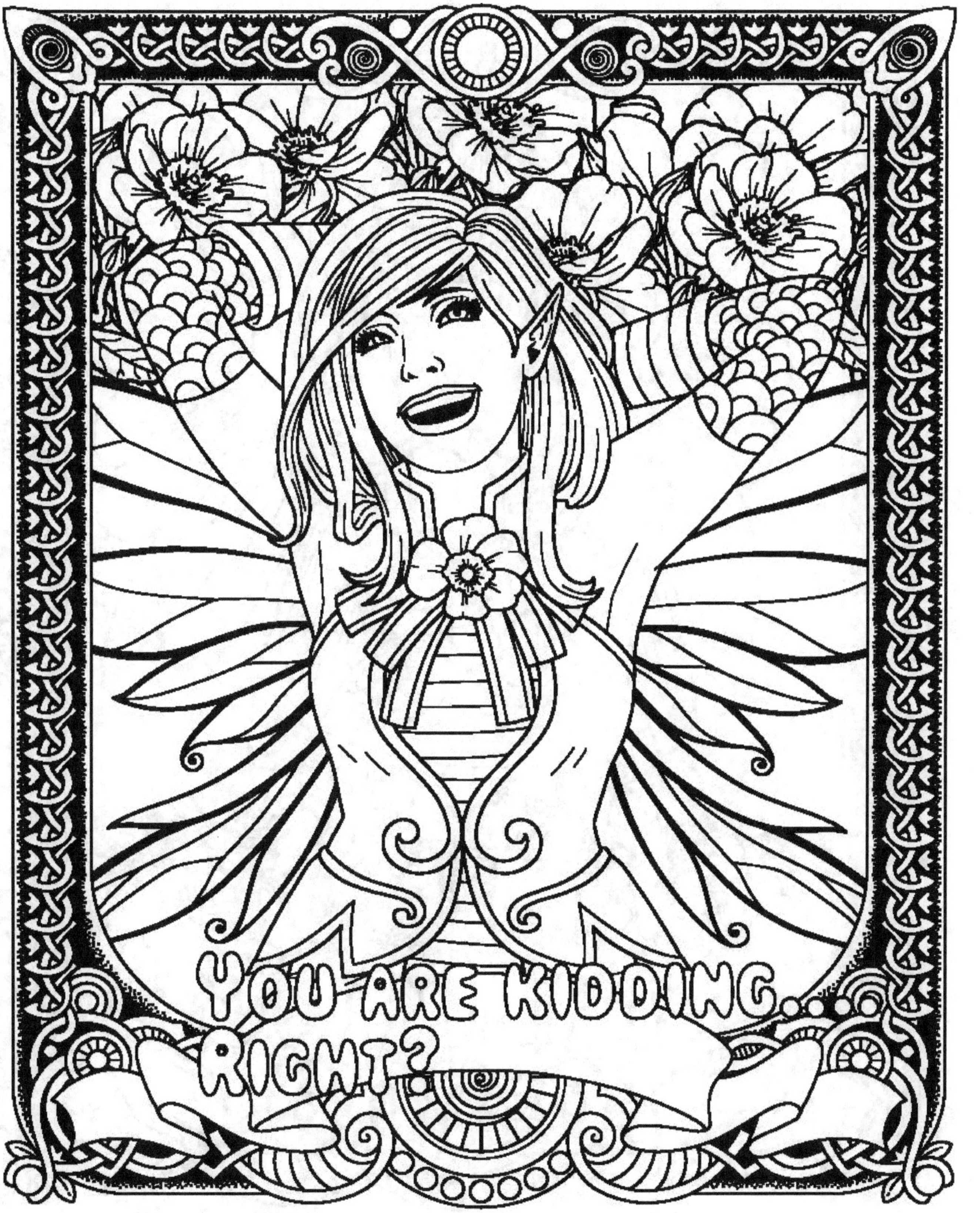
YOU ARE KIDDING...
RIGHT?

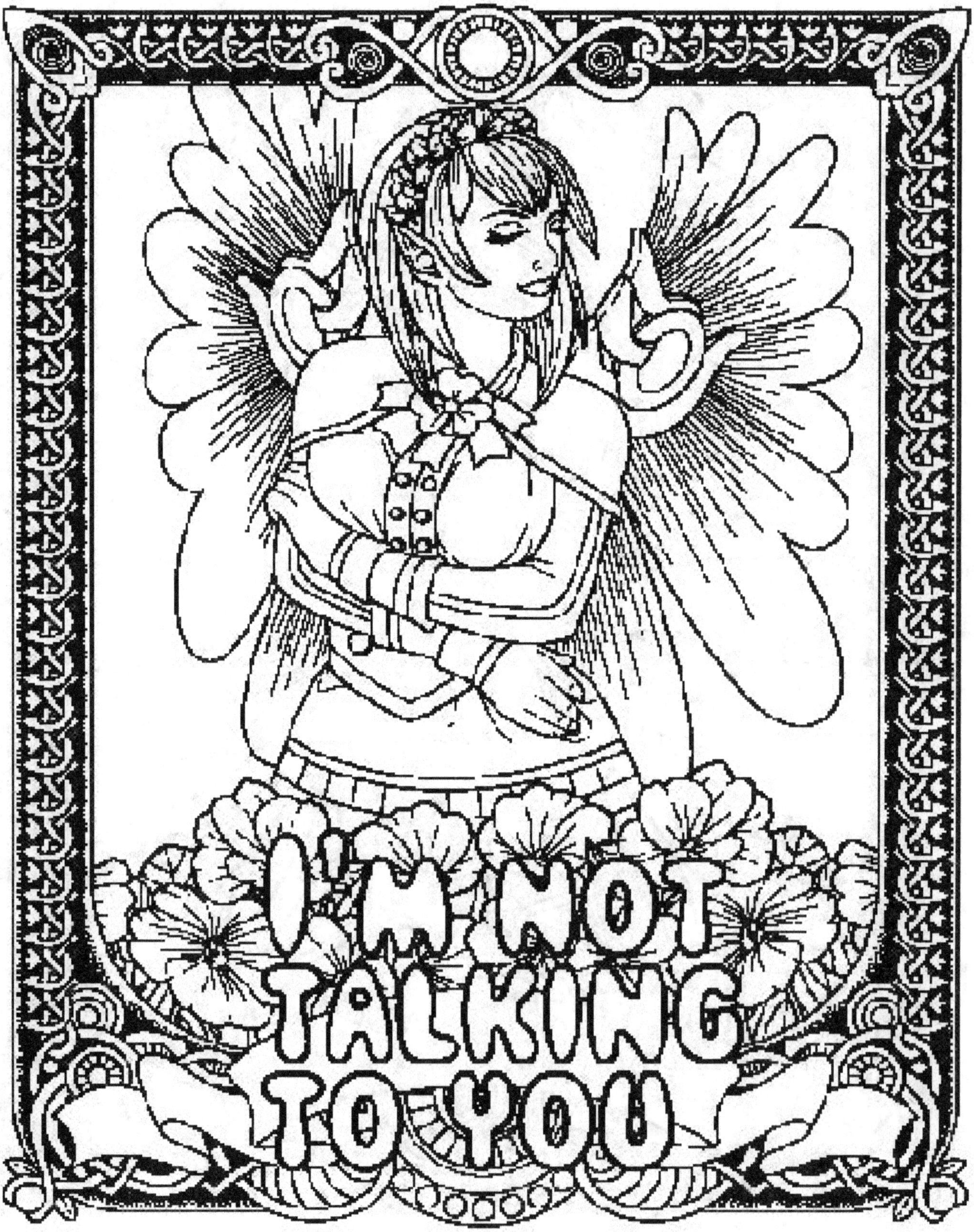
I'M NOT
TALKING
TO YOU

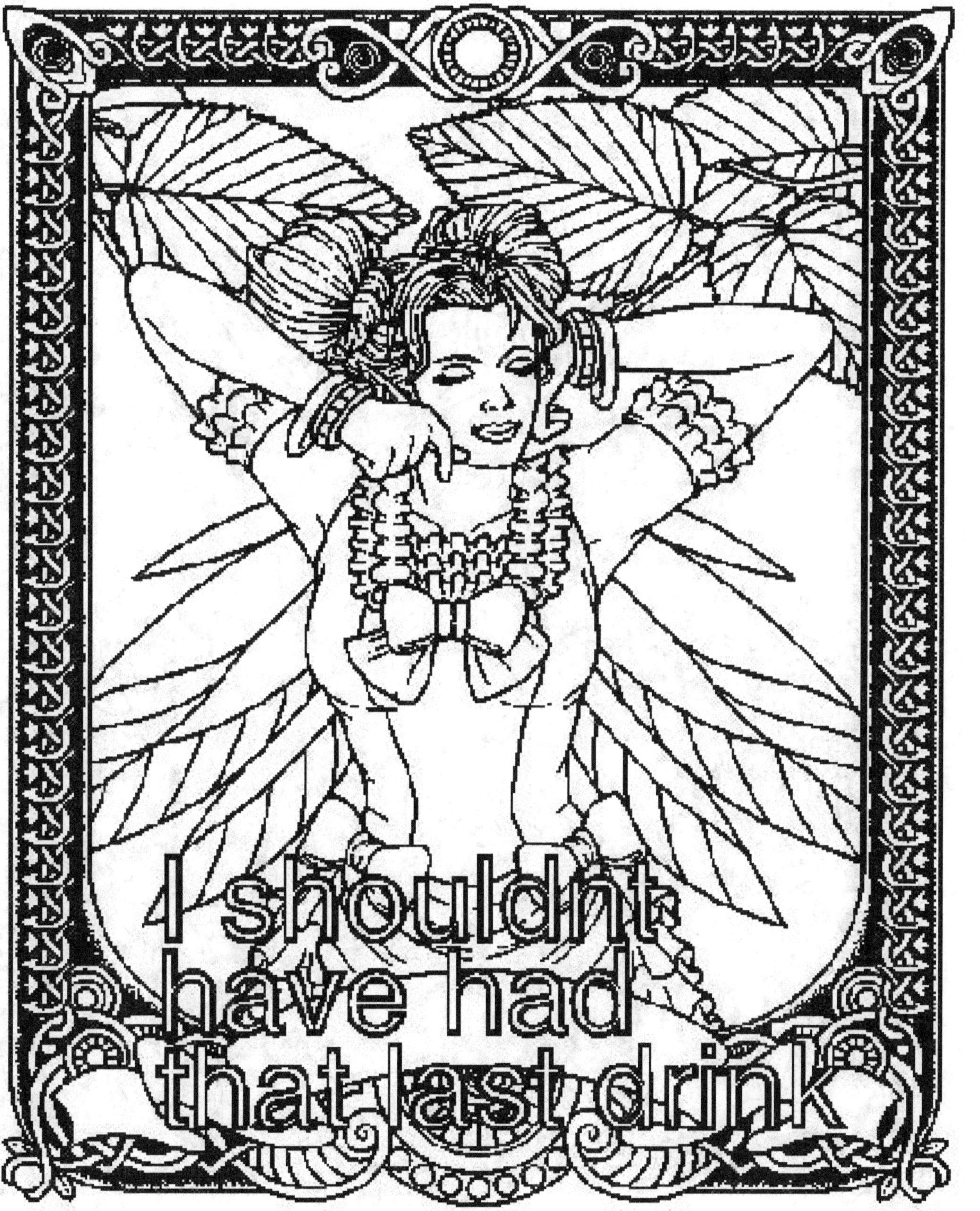
I shouldnt have had that last drink

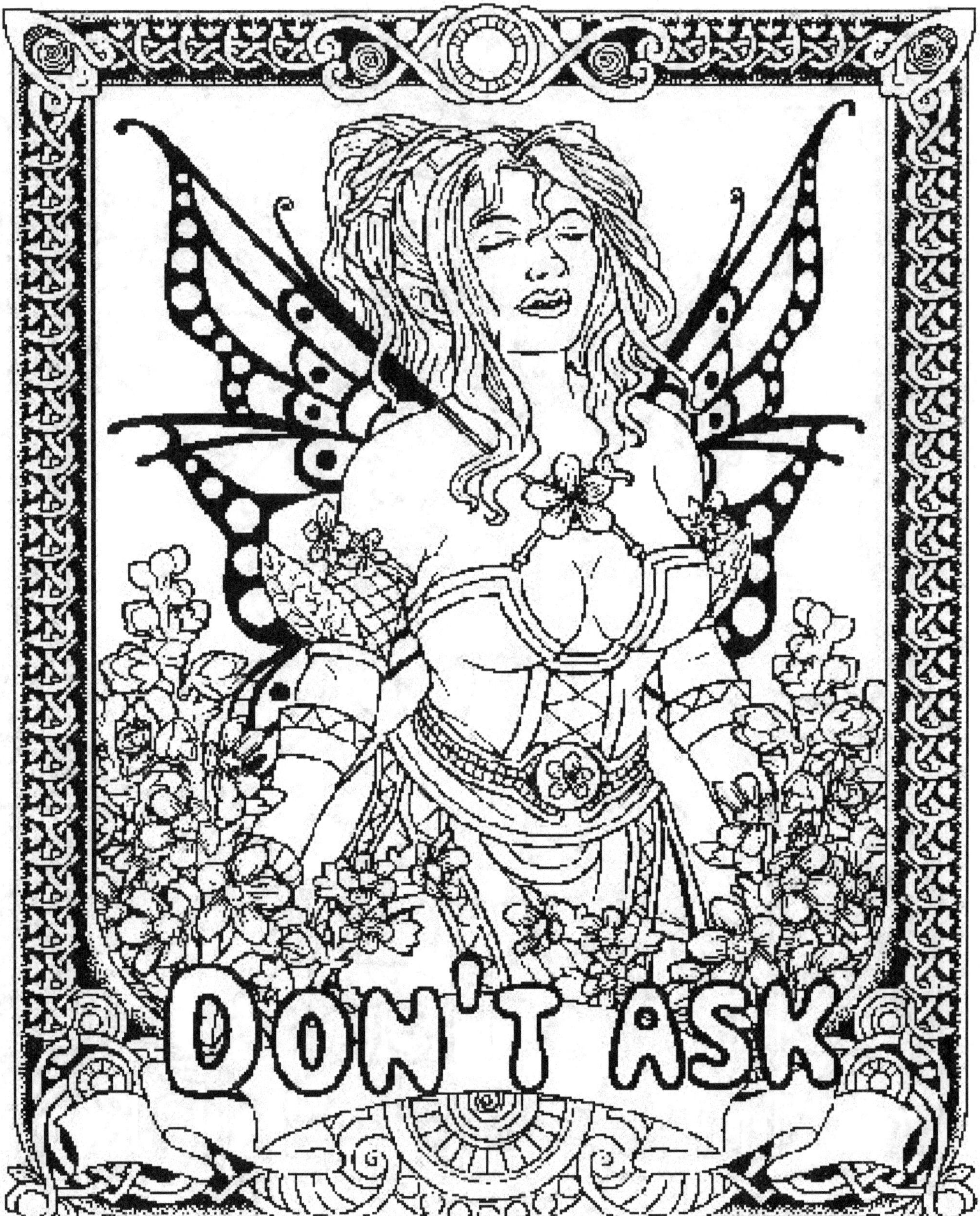
DON'T ASK

www.ingramcontent.com/pod-product-compliance
Lightning Source LLC
Chambersburg PA
CBHW081526220526
45467CB00010B/3069
9798709426696